At Home in the
English Countryside

At Home in the English Countryside

DESIGNERS AND THEIR DOGS

Susanna Salk

Foreword by Nina Campbell

Photography by Stacey Bewkes

RIZZOLI
NEW YORK

New York · Paris · London · Milan

Table of Contents

Foreword
by Nina Campbell

DOGS SEEM TO BE AN INTEGRAL part of design—after all, they come in the most incredible designs themselves. And, much like creating a room, sometimes the most surprising mixture delivers the most interesting result. Dogs also seem to have an innate sense of taste. My Theo always chooses not only the most comfortable chair or sofa but also goes unerringly to what becomes a best-selling fabric when I am working in my fabric studio. He is there to share the euphoria of a design installation that has gone brilliantly or just to wait patiently by my side when some problems— not to mention long travel days—can leave me exhausted.

Behind so many of the best designers is a dog waiting to welcome them home. That wonderful, loyal friend curls up with you and shares your life. An Englishman's home is his castle, but his dog is his best friend. Throughout history dogs have been portrayed with their masters, from the grandest King Charles with his spaniels to the more mundane but still much-loved mutt. Somehow an English country house is not a home without dogs, as you will see in this enchanting book.

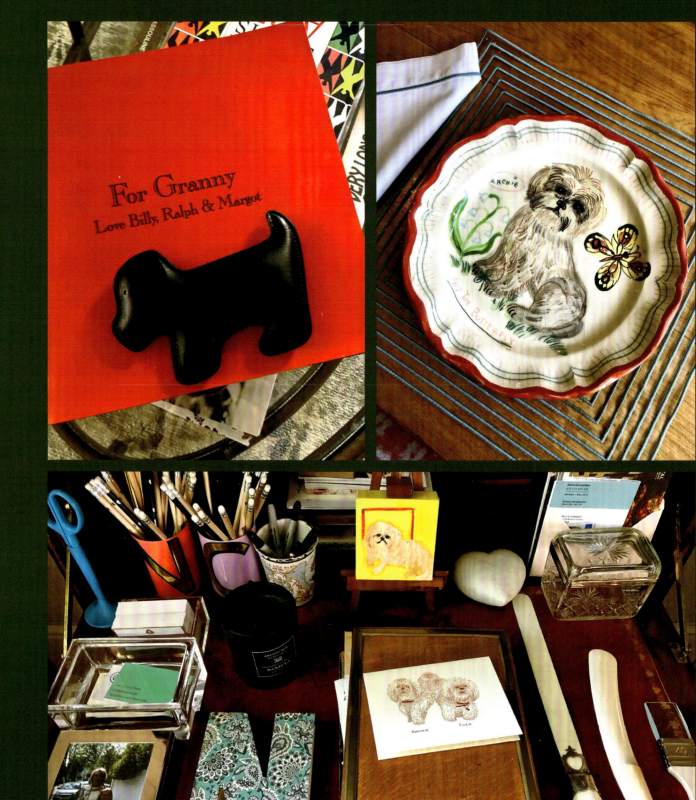

Introduction
by Susanna Salk

"YOU'VE GOT A LONG JOURNEY ahead, don't you, ladies," proclaimed the rental car gentleman, handing me my keys. His jolly yet concerned English lilt pushed his words into more of a statement than a question. My photographer, Stacey Bewkes, and I were only traveling for eight days across the English countryside to shoot the British companion to our previous book, *At Home with Dogs and Their Designers*, which focuses on American-based designers, but our far-reaching and ambitious timetable, and the fact that I would be driving for the first time on the opposite side of the road, meant that we might as well have been setting out on a *Lord of the Rings* kind of adventure.

We learned how to program the car's GPS so that our first destination—a country home with an address that spanned two lines with poetic ambiguity—could be found by simply inserting the extensive postal code's last few digits and letters. This tip thrust the destination into sharp focus and with the accompanying British female voice of the GPS, whose almost impatient tone was appreciated given my hesitation and jet lag, we lurched out of the parking lot and were on our way. Stacey was an invaluable copilot to my left, using her reassuring voice and distinct hand gestures to indicate that, while we were turning right we actually needed to keep to the left. After two blocks, we merged shakily into London's early morning rush and ultimately out of the city.

This trip took more than a year of planning. We met with eight UK design stars and their beloved dogs at their country homes in eight days (the remaining more garden-centric nine were shot the following spring) across different parts of the English countryside. All were more or less a two-hour drive from London, our home base.

Trains did not afford us the flexibility to zip from one home to another in a day or straight back to London for another appointment, and almost all of the homes were a good driving distance from the nearest stations. There were few conveniently located inns in between.

As daunting as our itinerary and deadline seemed, we just had to accept the challenge. As dog and design lovers, we had relished the year spent photographing designers and their dogs in some of the most beautiful homes and gardens in the United States. A sequel came calling and our focus was drawn immediately across the pond. It is not that the French or the Italians do not adore their dogs . . . but there is something inextricably intertwined between the British countryside and dogs. One immediately conjures up a cozy *World of Interiors* image full of chintz, corgis, Wellies, and faded roses. The truth is that and so much more.

11

About ninety minutes and almost twenty pesky roundabouts later, Stacey and I pulled up to the charming home of Carlos Sánchez-García in scenic Norfolk. It was right out of a storybook, complete with weathered gate, creamy gravel, and ivy stretching across the redbrick facade. Suddenly the daunting prospect of what lay ahead—capturing the intimate and stylish lives of these designers, none of whom we had met before, not to mention their pups—silenced our usual chatter.

Before I had even gotten out of the car, a wonderful little mottled mutt named Alfred jumped into my lap and sat there, while I took a moment to collect my confidence. There was something about the warmth of Alfred, as well as his unbridled trust and joy, that made me feel at home. I handed Stacey her camera bag, then carried Alfred inside where Sánchez-García was waiting for us with tea.

We spent the next week meeting, shooting, and ogling an array of dogs, from lurchers to terriers, seniors to pups, in a variety of stunning country homes—from converted barns to Jacobean manors—with gardens featuring everything from greenhouses full of pink geraniums to endless beds of dahlias. We shot dog collars, one of custom leather and green malachite, and dog bowls of antique Spode porcelain. Upon arrival we were offered tea, of course, but also champagne, fresh pressed apple cider, homemade quiche and quince jam, and elderflower cordials. We even received a dinner invitation to Annabel's in London. We accepted all with pleasure.

The designers' birth countries range from New Zealand to Italy to Spain, but all of their fashionable feet are firmly planted in Britain's soil for the long run. They design projects all over the world and manage bustling offices in London and yet crave the sanctity of their country retreats. They believe deeply that each piece in their homes tells a story, be it a grand seventeenth-century Flemish tapestry or a humble teapot. And their dogs. One was obsessed with my shiny black rain boot and would not let it go, to the point where I had to do the shoot barefoot. Another snuggled alongside me as I took a breather to call home. Another sat like a duchess when we were ready to shoot and then ran unconstrained through the surrounding fields of wildflowers. Still another ate all the power bars I had stashed in my bag when no one was looking. They all, needless to say, were perfect.

Along the way Stacey was always my North Star, reminding me to keep left after every turn, especially on the narrow country lanes. For this left-hander sometimes it just proved too much after a long day, so we mutually agreed to make a thirty-minute detour to visit a shop we had read about in *Vogue*. Whenever I spotted yet another dazzling country vista unfolding as we came around a bend or a particularly beguiling tablescape, thinking that we should shoot it, Stacey would cheerfully chime in, "Already got it."

We have been on many far-flung trips together, and this was the longest one. Yet it was the only one where we looked at each other over our suitcases and admitted that we would have happily stayed longer, for all of the dogs had made us feel at home. And that is what dogs do best.

Anouska Hempel, William, and Wattle

DESIGNER
Anouska Hempel
Interior designer

DOGS
William, age eight
Italian whippet

Wattle, age eight
Italian whippet

THEIR COUNTRY HOME
Shaw
Bath, England

SHAW, A QUEEN ANNE HOUSE, was found by accident five years ago after Anouska Hempel and her husband, financier Sir Mark Weinberg, were in a local pub in the area when a stranger—recognizing Hempel—told her about a wonderful old house with a magnificent driveway for sale nearby. "There wasn't a moat, but there was a ha-ha and a long row of trees. This was going to be a glorious spot to experiment with my landscape ideas," says Hempel.

The celebrated antipodean-born designer's vision is far-reaching and renowned, from yachts, including her own, to flagship stores, such as Louis Vuitton in Paris, Henry Cotton's in Milan for Moncler, and Van Cleef & Arpels worldwide, as well as a private villa in Switzerland and a palace in Istanbul with a twenty-acre Mogul garden. Her design for London's Blakes Hotel put it on the map as the world's first luxury boutique hotel.

"Landscapes are my passion. It is the inside and outside that bring the whole of life together," says Hempel. "I love working, and inspiration comes day and night. My eye sees everything."

Weekdays the Weinbergs live in Ennismore Gardens in London, in a home inspired by Dutch canal houses, with an interior of black lacquer and conceived, as Hempel describes, "like a journey, almost as a rite of passage into an exotic world of imagination. It is Japanese high camp."

Journeying to the country house is equally inventive, starting with the mode of transportation, which for the dogs is inside a horse box, complete with a mattress in the back and picnic baskets. The approach to Shaw is lined with hundred-year-old elm trees and benches equally ancient. "We love to sit on them and take in the magnificence of the wheat fields beyond," says Hempel.

The garden below the house is equally transportive, with its ha-ha, derelict folly, ancient brick walls, and trail of 'Kiftsgate' roses rambling all the way to the front door. Hempel likes to "topiarize" everything, even though the process can take years to create the specific structure she envisions, such as a hedge or maze. Her patience has reaped an intricate topiary of hornbeams that guide you into a series of squared-up courtyards along with catalpa trees and pollarded square mulberry in the shape of huge leafy umbrellas.

On the rise above, the house sits, proudly elegant. Much of the year drooping wisteria hugs its Bath stone walls, and its scent, combined with nearby jasmine and datura, makes for intoxicating perfume in the early spring. "It is Japan and Italy in the English countryside," says Hempel.

The dogs sleep in their own bedroom in rattan dog baskets. Their meals are often crunchy dog croutons along with braised oxtail served in Goyard bowls. Dog guests are unfortunately not encouraged due to the presence of two very old Burmese cats.

One of Hempel's favorite pastimes is to watch the whippets go wild, running about the property. "To see them so free and happy is just great." In preparation for their energetic scampering, sometimes she wraps the dogs' delicate ankles in black ribbon à la Chanel to prevent scratching, since they chase each other through the hedgerows perhaps in search of rabbits. "These dogs are my best friends and are the symbols of my free time and the magic of country life."

The lady of the manor, Hempel, reposes with William and Wattle beneath hanging wisteria in the back garden.

RIGHT: The Queen Anne house is fashioned from Bath stone and is surrounded by pollarded plane trees. An overhanging beech affords the house a decorative evergreen warmth.

ABOVE: In the dining room, a painting of a pert Pomeranian hangs above a Bakelite cocktail shaker, Japanese paper fans, and Scottish Baronial snuffboxes made of antlers.

OPPOSITE: Just steps from the entrance hall, visitors are greeted with a colorful circa 1902 Victorian tiled floor and inviting plantation chairs covered with Turkish tapestry cushions coupled with black and tan lamps. The black lacquer screens give a sense of mystery to what lies beyond.

FOLLOWING SPREAD: William and Wattle lounge on an ebony Anglo-Indian settee. Near the Japanese screen are pairs of torchière and Anouska Hempel Design jousting poles with tan grosgrain ribbon, as well as various Japanese hatboxes and porphyry bowls.

William and Wattle stand at the top of the gray and white staircase near a painting,
which includes an Irish wolfhound and a whippet.

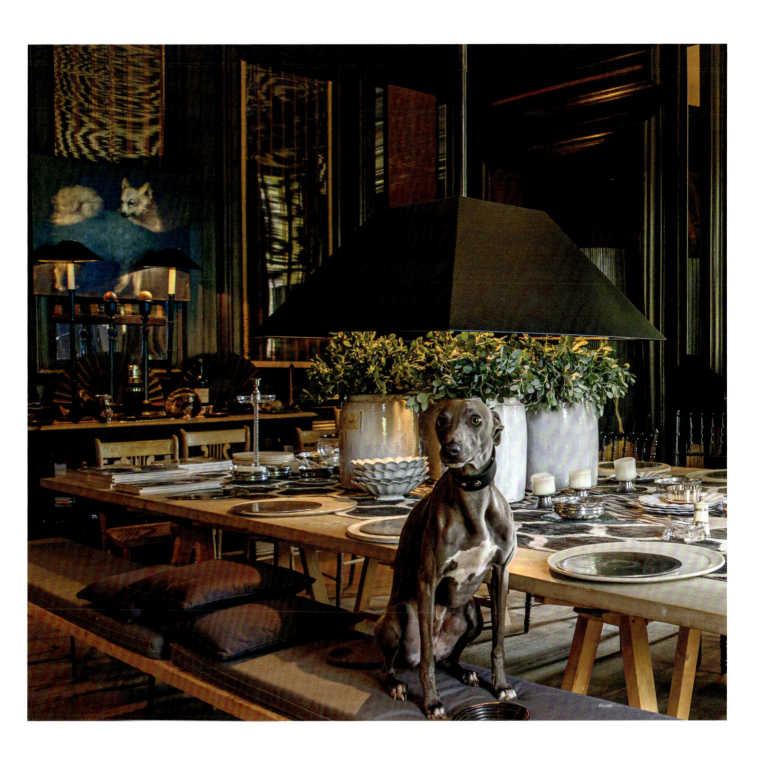

William sits at the trestle table in the dining room that is festooned with large ceramic pots filled with olive branches. The white marble chargers and pewter plates are from Anouska Hempel Design.

The Dutch-style circa 1711 house is fashioned out of Bath stone. Wattle poses in front of the continuous rows of hornbeams.

Bridget Elworthy, Henrietta Courtauld, Iris, and Arthur

DESIGNERS
Bridget Elworthy and
Henrietta Courtauld
*Landscape designers
and founders of
The Land Gardeners*

DOGS
Iris, age eight
Labrador Retriever

Arthur, age nine
*Long-haired
Jack Russell terrier*

THEIR COUNTRY HOME
Wardington Manor
Oxfordshire, England

THE ENTRANCE TO WARDINGTON MANOR, just a few hours northwest of London in Oxfordshire, does its best to stay humble. Visitors are cautioned by a faded sign to go "very slow" for dogs and horses, and the Jacobean house reveals itself shyly, set back behind rust-hued gateposts and accessed by a short driveway off the village lane. Its unremarkable side entrance defers to the gravel courtyard with its array of wheelbarrows, tractors, and even the odd pony.

But just a few steps into this sixteenth-century structure fashioned from Horton stone, which was later combined with Arts and Crafts–style reconfigurations in the twenties, one realizes that this is no ordinary country house. There is an explosion of flowers throughout the property: many magnificent cutting gardens are surrounded by high hedges, which have been topiarized into exotic birds. When one steps inside the out-door entry hall, dazzling blooms continue everywhere, whether merrily clustered in buckets waiting to be arranged or already in romantic bouquets that reflect just the right amount of human touch, from pale pink Japanese anemones in antique silver cups to scarlet dahlias in old Fulham Pottery vases.

Walking past the beautiful plasterwork of chevron zigzags and pastoral friezes into the double-height library with its paneled walls displaying rare books, the Arts and Crafts fireplace, and worn chintz armchairs in pale pinks and blues, is to be transported to an enchanted past where time moves as leisurely as the tendrils of wisteria twining around the loggia in early summer. This has been Bridget Elworthy's home for the past ten years, which she shares with her husband, Forbes Elworthy, and their three children. Her business partner, Henrietta Courtauld, who lives in London with her husband, Toby Courtauld, comes up regularly as Wardington is also the base of The Land Gardeners' operations.

Elworthy and Courtauld are always followed by their faithful and friendly dogs Iris, an eight-year-old black Labrador who belongs to Elworthy, and Arthur, a nine-year-old long-haired Jack Russell who belongs to Courtauld. The women launched their gardening business in 2013, and the dogs spend each working moment at their sides either here or in their Notting Hill design studio in London.

Elworthy and Courtauld don stylishly practical work uniforms of navy linen smocks, with generous pockets etched with The Land Gardeners' monogram, over leggings and leather jodhpur boots. Activities such as turning microbial aerobic compost, teaching ardent followers about healthy soil, restoring walled gardens for clients from France to Zimbabwe, or ferrying organically grown blooms into some of London's toniest homes and boutiques keep this working duo busy. "We design productive gardens that are wild, romantic, and joyful," says Elworthy, who met Courtauld when their children attended the same nursery school a dozen years ago.

Throughout it all, Iris the Labrador, so named because Elworthy always wanted to name a daughter Iris, and Arthur the long-haired Jack Russell, named after King Arthur from Tintagel Castle on the edge of Bodmin Moor in Cornwall where he was born, aid the business as best they can, whether digging holes in the garden or helping keep the muntjacs away. Whatever the task, the dogs are close collaborators like their human owners. Sometimes they are joined by Phlox, the working cocker spaniel belonging to the head gardener, who loves to play tag with a gardening glove in her mouth.

Well-earned dog biscuits for Arthur and Iris are served in white enamel bowls in the large kitchen with its cream-colored AGA stove and stone flooring. Nap time finds Iris and Arthur in a dog basket in The Land Gardeners' seed room.

If the weather and wet paws bring in mud, Elworthy does not fuss about the occasional print across the rush matting or the time-worn Persian rugs. "We're not too worried about making a mess here," she says.

The two women like to start their day in the country at the very heart of their business with the dogs by their sides. "It is very good for you to walk around your garden first thing in the morning with your dog," says Courtauld. "It is a moment of quiet for us before the day begins." When dusk arrives, the dogs are still close at hand. Adds Elworthy, "They are such loyal and constant companions."

PREVIOUS SPREAD: Bridget Elworthy (left) and Henrietta Courtauld of The Land Gardeners cut dahlias from one of the splendid cutting gardens at Wardington Manor, with a little help from Phlox, the working cocker spaniel who belongs to the head gardener. This is home base to their thriving gardening business and also where Elworthy lives with her family. "Bridget and I design wild, joyful, and productive gardens," says Courtauld.

RIGHT: During their workday at Wardington Manor, Elworthy and Courtauld make time to take the dogs for a runabout. Here, looking past the gate-posts built in rust-hued ironstone across to the main cutting garden. The unusual bird topiary dates from the 1930s.

OPPOSITE: The manor's hall boasts plasterwork from the 1920s with chevron zigzags and Jacobean-style pastorals bearing images of fruit-blooming boughs and serpents among spring flowers.

ABOVE: In the flower room, Arthur and Iris are often on hand while Courtauld and Elworthy arrange the garden's bounty for The Land Gardeners' weekly deliveries to London.

RIGHT: Since The Land Gardeners' office is above the library, Arthur often visits it from the old limed wood staircase.

BELOW: Simple botanical paintings from old markets line the flower room walls along with vases of all shapes and sizes.

OPPOSITE AND FOLLOWING SPREAD: The paneled library was created for Lord Wardington in the 1920s for his rare book collections. The seventeenth-century limed wood paneling was brought in when the library was remodeled in the 1920s from Theydon Bois in Essex. Hodsell and Mackenzie chintz from Soane Britain are paired with simple unlined linen curtains.

OPPOSITE: Iris in the smoke room, a cozy wood-paneled room with a fire. This is where the family congregates in the winter.

ABOVE: Old shredded crewelwork provides an elegant backdrop to the inner hall, where a drinks tray next to the grand piano is ready for guests. The rush matting beneath the piano is often littered with half-chewed dog bones.

RIGHT: Frequently used croquet mallets stand ready next to a cabinet filled with the family's old glass Christmas tree decorations.

FOLLOWING SPREAD: In the kitchen, a cream AGA and stone flooring are cheerful companions to an open shelving system that casually displays everything from tableware and trays to artwork and a flower cutting or two.

RIGHT: Courtauld wears The Land Gardeners' daily uniform of a navy canvas smock. Its deep pockets hold everything from secateurs to seeds, freeing a hand to hold a dog leash.

BELOW: The Jacobean structure, fashioned from Horton stone in the seventeenth century, was later altered with Arts and Crafts–style reconfigurations in the twenties.

OPPOSITE: "Bridget and I design wild, joyful, and productive gardens," says Courtauld. Here, they are joined by Phlox, the working cocker spaniel, who belongs to the head gardener and aptly plays with a gardening glove.

Bunny Guinness, Grace Jones, Beetle, and Dollar

DESIGNER
Bunny Guinness
*Landscape architect
and journalist*

DOGS
Grace Jones, age seven
Jack Russell terrier

Beetle, age seven
Jack Russell terrier

Dollar, age seven
Jack Russell terrier

THEIR COUNTRY HOME
*Cambridgeshire,
England*

"WE HAVE A RATHER TOO dog-friendly house," says Bunny Guinness with a pleased smile, of the circa 1300s manor house she shares with three dogs (one belongs to her daughter, Unity, who brings her dog to work at the bustling home office on the grounds) and her husband, Kevin Guinness. "There are dog baskets or rugs in most rooms, usually by the fire."

The tiny original structure came complete with a thirteenth-century vaulted undercroft, and an eighteenth-century farmhouse was later built around it. "I love homes that are arranged around a courtyard, because you feel protected," says Guinness, an internationally renowned garden designer who travels as far away as Asia to implement her talents and is a regular panelist on BBC radio, not to mention a six-time gold medalist at the Chelsea Flower Show. Guinness has completely converted the once dilapidated eight acres of grounds over the thirty-three years she has lived there into a verdant paradise, complete with main courtyards, vegetable and children's gardens, orchard, and pool garden, with twin avenues of pleached hornbeam arched overhead offering delicious shade. She even planted, sometimes from cuttings, a thousand grand trees that now shelter the property from winter's cold winds. "I took two weeks off from work to plant them," says Guinness. "Some were only a foot high at the time and my husband thought I was crazy. Now all these years later he loves their protection." She was always intent on planting the multiple gardens to be seen from the house. "That's the only way they will properly be appreciated and used," says Guinness, who designed the kitchen windows to be at a lower level so the kitchen garden could be better viewed from inside. "It means that we and the dogs can pretty nearly always find somewhere that is sheltered and sunny at any time." Inside, all the reception rooms have fireplaces. "We love hunkering down by a fire on cold winter evenings, enjoying the smell of woodsmoke, and basking in the warmth," says Guinness. The dogs mainly sleep in their Charley Chau beds in the kitchen. "They can snuggle down inside these, quite hidden," she says. "A dog psychologist once told me that dogs feel that, as you are their masters, they are on duty when you are with them. In a snuggle bed, they can avoid eye contact and relax."

Beetle is from a litter up the road and was brought into the family fold as company for Grace Jones, who had a habit of jumping into vans with deliverymen. "She would jump in when they were not looking and they often did not find her until miles up the road. Having Beetle around has helped break that habit," says Guinness. As soon as Unity and her dog Dollar arrive each work morning, Dollar nudges Beetle and Grace Jones from their baskets with gusto to play, giving Unity time to focus on designing gardens, liaising with clients, and dealing with contractors.

At mealtime, the dogs eat raw meat, leftover scraps, and vegetables from the garden; Guinness never buys commercial dog food. "Grace Jones has a very eclectic palate and particularly loves licking the mixing bowl once I have removed the cake mixture," says Guinness.

The trio works up an appetite by following Guinness on her daily rounds as she feeds her extensive menagerie of Oxford Sandy and Black pigs in the chic stone pigsty she fashioned. Soay sheep, Dexter cattle, guinea fowl, and chickens come rain or snow. "The dogs love the routine," says Guinness, "especially teasing and barking at the pigs, who think they are a joke." When the garden has an orphaned lamb, the dogs snuggle in the straw next to Guinness while she bottle-feeds it throughout the night.

As relaxed as Guinness is about their whereabouts (the dogs come and go as they please via a cat flap or dog door), she is strict about their staying out of the flower beds. "I always spend a day gardening with new dogs when they are puppies, and every time I step into a flower bed they follow me, so I say 'no' gently and lift them back off the bed. At the end of the day they have learned not to go on the flower borders. You cannot have a great garden if your dogs spend their lives rooting in your flower beds." While the property has been a constant source of work for Guinness, she has never been daunted by any of it, whether repairing the roofs, or making sure the dogs do not chase too many rabbits down their holes. "It seems to be the sort of house that just gives and gives the more you get to know it," says Guinness. "I feel that part of me is part of it."

PREVIOUS SPREAD: Dollar supervises Bunny pruning the 'Thomas Edison' dahlias and the 'Sensation Mixed' cosmos in the border that edges the courtyard in front of the thirteenth-century farmhouse.

RIGHT: Bunny designed and built the front courtyard garden from scratch. The sheltered private space formed an outdoor playpen for dogs and children when they were tiny. The quince trees have beautiful early foliage, fabulous flowers, and golden fruit. This garden is seen from much of the house throughout the year, and as such, the planting changes dramatically with every season.

ABOVE: Grace Jones waits in the yard ready to welcome visitors: she is the most sociable dog and adores men in big vans and has been known to stow away with them, only to be discovered miles from home. The boxwood adds structure to the main yard, which is kept fairly simple, and the massive stone barns add a wonderful agricultural feel.

OPPOSITE: The main front door to the house opens onto the hallway, which has, like every reception room in the house, a huge fireplace. Old stone flags and worn rugs furnish the floors. Every reception room has at least one doorway leading to the garden, and in the warmer months they are usually wide open to take in the views, while fresh air streams into the house.

OPPOSITE: In the partially walled garden, Guinness planted double rows of hornbeam trees as sticks just a foot high and now they frame a central axis, directing the view toward the open countryside and totally screening the intrusive building to the right. The pool was also added, bringing in a myriad of wildlife: woodpeckers, frogs, newts, dragonflies, and scores of birds. It is a water source for Guinness's bees.

ABOVE: Grace Jones is a sun worshipper who follows the sun around the yard picking the most sheltered and sunniest spots. Here she catches a catnap outside Guinness's daughter Unity's office door.

A crucial part of each workday is when Guinness's daughter, Unity, who works in Guinness's design office next to the house, schedules playtime with the dogs. Here Unity's dog, Dollar, aims high while Grace Jones assesses the situation. The topiary is homegrown, and the pot it is planted in has no base, so the plant roots through to the ground and thus does not need watering or feeding.

ABOVE: Dollar loves trotting around the garden checking on any stray rabbits, moles, or even foxes. The doors adjacent to her lead into the walled garden from the nuttery. The hazel boughs are trained over a metal framework and box balls frame the entrance.

RIGHT: The AGA is appreciated as much by the dogs as by the people. The gentle heat is not just used for all the cooking but also for air-drying washing, warming wet and cold dogs, storing collars, and drying herbs and produce.

OPPOSITE: The wicker dog baskets handily stack on top of each other, allowing one leaf of the French door to open. Grace Jones loves the top deck because it affords her an ideal view of the rabbits in the far field beyond. The lime green cushions in the beds have big pockets, letting the dogs nestle inside, which they adore. They are made by charleychau.com.

Carlos Sánchez-García, Theodora, Tristan, and Alfie

DESIGNER
Carlos Sánchez-García
Interior designer

DOGS
Theodora Oriane Cécile
de Beaulieu, age nine
Whippet

Tristan Peregrine
Sebastian d'Arundel,
age eight
Whippet

Alfred (often called
Alfie), age seven
*A mongrel cross
between a pug and
a chihuahua*

THEIR COUNTRY HOME
Baconsthorpe
North Norfolk, England

IT'S NOT OFTEN THAT dogs are lucky enough to receive lyrically long names inspired by iconic figures in music and literature and a beloved family uncle, but Theodora Oriane Cécile de Beaulieu, Tristan Peregrine Sebastian d'Arundel, and Alfred more than live up to their unique callings in the country. They eat out of limited-edition antique Spode porcelain bowls, sleep on cushions made with vintage Welsh blankets stuffed with feathers, fully covered with tartan rugs, and sport leather collars hand-stitched by a local craftsman, cushioned with soft lambskin. And yet life is never too precious to sneak into the utility room and cause havoc by raiding desserts set aside for the night's dinner party. It is all in a glorious day in the country.

"We were not particularly looking for a weekend house," says Carlos Sánchez-García, having lived in London with his partner, Michael Newman, for the past nineteen years. "When we arrived, the lady who showed us around the house welcomed us with a bag of wild mushrooms she had picked. She handed over the keys and told us to leave them under a pot when we had finished. Then she left. As we opened the door, Theodora and Tristan ran wild up and down. That's when Michael and I knew the house was meant to be ours."

It is a quintessentially English early seventeenth-century manor farmhouse within the Barningham Estate, on a remarkably quiet bend of a narrow country lane, near the village church, surrounded by farmland. The main body of the house has a beautifully checkered brick facade, with original glazed roof tiles. The eighteenth-century extension was built in vernacular flint. "From the outset I was determined that the house look as if it had always been decorated that way," says Sánchez-García, who has had his own design practice in London since 2008. He achieves this with a careful yet playful mix of antique furniture and textiles from different periods, with heavy Eastern influences. "I added pattern and texture to the rooms to give that indispensable generational layering so inherent to the English country house." A nineteenth-century Djizak Suzani from Uzbekistan, antique cushions in vintage silk velvet ikats (bought on his travels to Istanbul) to curtains in a print velvet fabric by Robert Kime (with an almost two-meter repeat) to a bedcover (handmade of raised roses and crocheted bullionlike fringe), and a window seat with vintage Colefax & Fowler chintz are just a few examples.

Layering proves a literal necessity in the house. Sánchez-García put rush matting over the original stone and pament flooring to protect from the cold. He added a backdrop tapestry in the dining room to pad the very old walls. This room has no electricity, so lucky party guests are lit by candlelight.

The kitchen, which was the original tack room, hosts "one of those quintessentially British institutions without which my life would not be the same," says Sánchez-García of his AGA stove. "It keeps the kitchen constantly warm, including the dogs. They would not sleep anywhere

else unless there's a roaring fire on." Antique pottery, such as plates from France, Scottish spongeware, and Eastern European bowls, are stacked nearby. Sánchez-García and Newman also love to fill the pantry with homemade jams and chutneys, which they prepare on weekends. "It is not only therapeutic, but it uses all the produce we have in the garden, from blackberries to plums, and it sorts out all those Christmas presents." says Sánchez-García.

In the snug, a jewel box of a study, complete with an ottoman covered in an antique Qashqai blanket, Sánchez-García commissioned a special fireplace from a local artist to honor, through a set of handmade and painted Delft tiles, the bright parts of the family's life in the country—from their church to dahlias, Mocha ware, tulips, the owl that lives in their barn, and most especially, Theodora and Tristan. Alfred came to the family after it was completed, having first belonged to Newman's late mother, who became too ill to care for him.

The now trio adore the sense of freedom they have in the country. "It's noticeable in their faces," says Sánchez-García. "And Michael and I feel the same way. The dogs are part of our life here and use every part of the house just as we do. Is there any other way?"

PREVIOUS SPREAD: Sánchez-García and his whippets, Theodora and Tristan, always greet a day in the country with equal zest. The original seventeenth-century flooring was recently discovered under a heavy layer of concrete and tar and restored to its original condition. Rush matting over the original stone and pament flooring protects paws from the cold and adds texture.

LEFT: Nestled on a quiet bend of a narrow country lane, the main body of the seventeenth-century manor farmhouse has a beautifully checkered brick facade, with original glazed roof tiles. Despite being nearly four hundred years old, the manor farmhouse exterior was in good condition and so Sánchez-García opted for a gentle intervention, merely repainting windows and doors, thus maintaining its character and idio-syncrasy. The front door and kitchen entrance are painted in Stiffkey Blue by Farrow & Ball, which takes its name from the nearby village of Stiffkey, where the salt marshes have a particular deep navy hue.

ABOVE: Sánchez-García's living room hosts antique furniture, including the William and Mary cabinet and textiles with heavy Eastern influences. "I wanted to add pattern and texture to the rooms as well as that indispensable generational layering so inherent to the English country house," says Sánchez-García. The sofa is covered with a nineteenth-century Djizak Suzani from Uzbekistan. The cushions are antique vintage silk velvet ikats bought on Sánchez-García's travels to Istanbul, as are the silk ikats on the handmade lampshade. The cushions were made by his local upholsterer.

RIGHT: The kitchen's cozy entry is kept snug with Sánchez-García's ingenious idea to hang a Robert Kime fabric on a handmade iron French pole and then line the lower part in leather to avoid fraying when rubbing over the pament. The nineteenth-century Hungarian bench is ideal for putting on boots and is lined with a French mattress made with a nineteenth-century Uzbek Suzani. A mélange of English chintz, antique Russian prints, and Suzani cushions ensure cheerful chic throughout the seasons.

OPPOSITE: Alfred enjoys refreshment from a limited-edition antique Spode porcelain bowl.

LEFT: Sánchez-García and the dogs like to retreat to the smallest room in the house on cold winter evenings. "This room is very informal and deeply personal," says Sánchez-García. "It features many of the things I cherish most: Eastern fabrics and sentimental objects." The ottoman is covered in an antique Qashqai blanket. The rug is antique Malayer. The table in between the Victorian armchairs is covered with an antique Uzbek kilim and draped over it is a Suzani with antique Uzbek tassels.

FOLLOWING SPREAD, LEFT: The master bedroom features an eighteenth-century Gillows four-poster bed, which Sánchez-García found while on a weekend break in the Lake District, with hangings made from Robert Kime's Tree Peony pattern, a favorite of Sánchez-García's.

FOLLOWING SPREAD, RIGHT: Tristan catches the afternoon sun in the main staircase, one of his preferred spots. The curtains behind are Algiers, a printed noil silk by Robert Kime.

OPPOSITE: "From the outset I was determined that the house look as if it had always been decorated this way," says Sánchez-García. The backdrop tapestry is a printed linen by Zardi and Zardi of Watts of Westminster, and the livery cupboard is seventeenth century as are the Delft vases and plates on it. "This room has no electrical light and is lit only by candles," says Sánchez-García. "Eighteen, to be precise."

ABOVE, LEFT: In Sánchez-García's living room, the mirror above the fireplace is eighteenth century, in the manner of William Kent. Two nineteenth-century Staffordshire dogs and a nineteenth-century Empire clock line the mantelpiece. "A fire is always the best place for a cup of tea after a long walk with the dogs," says Sánchez-García.

ABOVE, RIGHT: The skirted basin and roman blind are a thin-glazed linen chintz by Jean Monro, Bowness in Document. The nineteenth-century hand-colored prints add a splash of color to the walls. "No English country house is complete without birds, be they anywhere," says Sánchez-García.

RIGHT: In the blue dining room, Alfred crosses over the traditional rush matting, handwoven and hand-sewn locally using historical techniques. The textile on the chairs is Turkoman Stripe by Robert Kime, a subtle interpretation of a Turkoman kilim, chosen for its vibrant colors that complement the blue painted walls. The informal weave juxtaposes with the formal shape of the antique chairs.

ABOVE: Theodora and Tristan are never far from the constant warmth of the AGA stove in the house's kitchen, formerly a tack room. "It's one of those quintessentially British institutions without which my life would not be the same," says Sánchez-García, who loves to entertain as much as each weekend will allow.

OPPOSITE: Blackberries, blueberries, raspberries, gooseberries, quince jams, and chutneys, which Sánchez-García makes from his own garden, line the shelves in the pantry in the eighteenth-century extension. Largely untouched and adjacent to the kitchen, it seemed the perfect spot for a utility room. Practicality was the main objective. Hence there are open and skirted shelves for easy access and visibility of products. Walls are painted white and the woodwork in the same green as the kitchen walls next-door. The gingham is Small Suffolk in Peony by Ian Mankin. This is the only unheated room in the house. Radiators were removed so produce can keep fresh any time of the year.

FOLLOWING SPREAD: On the front lawn, the two-seater Regency bench is painted bright blue, and has a chintz cushion that complements the colors of delphiniums, cosmos, salvia, and verbena on the border behind it.

Christopher Howe, Apollo, and Great Bear

DESIGNER
Christopher Howe
*Designer and
antiques dealer*

DOGS
Apollo Slimline Hipster,
age five
Jack Russell terrier

Great Bear, age three
Maltipoo

THEIR COUNTRY HOME
Gloucestershire, England

NESTLED ALONGSIDE WILDFLOWERS AND a brook and tucked just off a country road, the stone barn that Christopher Howe converted and frequents is revealed across a cross section of staggered floors. Its four sections, separated by a generous oak staircase, deftly define all that is needed to enjoy a bucolic life in the country: a sitting room, kitchen, bedroom, and bathroom. "I push the glass doors wide open in the summer and the dogs can come and go, but also so that ducks can wander in, sometimes in the morning while I'm still in bed," says Howe. "Occasionally the sheep do, too."

As miniature in scale as the shelter appears, its limewashed raw-timber-clad walls, oak floors, and stone slabs—much of it salvaged and much of it crafted by local artisans—give a solid veritas to its existence. While Howe initially oversaw its construction in a speedy eight-and-a-half weeks on behalf of clients three years ago, whose main expansive house is nearer to London (and who let Howe use the barn while he restored a Baptist chapel in the nearby village for himself), its decor is decidedly slow-paced. There are thoughtful, intriguing choices, such as a 1950s Serge Mouille three-arm ceiling lamp hanging above a sixteenth-century bed from Yorkshire throughout. All the distinct yet humble pieces have been found for a song and bargained for here, there, and everywhere.

After all, Howe has an international reputation as an expert in the history of furniture. In 1986, this former sculpture student opened two bustling antiques and home shops on Pimlico Road: one called HOWE at 36 Bourne Street and the other HOWE London. Howe takes his ethos of mixing quality and character wherever he can. He created all the Irish paw foot benches at London's National Gallery that visitors flock to in order to have a brief respite.

The decor of the barn takes its style cues from Howe's belief that "most importantly I want to be surrounded by things I love and find useful." He comes here as often as he can, to enjoy the wildflowers in the summer and the crackling log fires during the bleak midwinter. He brings two dogs who are very much a part of his work family with him when their schedules allow—Apollo, who belongs to Joanne Brierley, his shop manager, and Great Bear, belonging to his daughter, Holly Howe, who also works with him. "During the workweek Apollo and Great Bear's principal duties include greeting customers at the shops and modeling," says Howe. He recently bought a farm in Sicily as another place to relax in warmth.

Howe's role for now with the dogs is more as a doting godparent. "I've had dogs since I was nine. Dotty, my beloved Jack Russell, died at age sixteen, three years ago. Everyone knew her along Pimlico Road— she was a connoisseur of upholstery and food, and we were inseparable, which is why now I just love looking after other people's dogs."

When Friday comes, the dogs and Howe head out of London and arise Saturday to take a walk to the quaint village a stone's throw away, including a visit to the post office; the local bakery, where they pick up their preordered loaf of bread; and church on Sunday morning at the fourteenth-century Norman chapel. When they return from their many adventures exploring the hills outside, Howe never frets about muddy paws within. "Everything especially on the ground floor is mud resistant," says Howe. "After all, the barn is in the middle of a field, so you can't be precious."

The sitting area's main sofa is covered in old army tent canvas and a worn Persian carpet. "It's self-cleaning," says Howe proudly. This is where he loves to peruse the racing newspaper often with Apollo and Great Bear at his side. In the Lilliputian entry, coat hooks are laden with various dog leads for different-sized dogs and coats and headgear for every type of weather. The dogs eat on the flagstone floor in the snug sunken kitchen. On top of the plain English cabinets are stoneware bowls filled with a local bounty of strawberries or eggs.

On Sunday they take the company van back to London with Apollo and Bear safely strapped in the front seat, recharged for the week ahead. When it comes to city or country living and welcoming dogs into your life, Howe's apt advice is as characteristically philosophical as instructional: "If you can own a dog then do; don't be too apprehensive but make a careful choice. Allow them to change your life for the better. You won't regret it as they'll teach you more about love and loyalty than you'll ever teach them."

PREVIOUS SPREAD: While at their Gloucestershire retreat, Howe and Great Bear make weekend time to stay updated on the latest news in the local *Racing Post*. "The sofa here is designed to take the muddy paws," says Howe. "I covered it in an old army tent canvas and a worn Persian carpet. It is self-cleaning."

RIGHT: The bucolic countryside is accessible with a simple push to open the glass doors, thanks to the ingenious layout Howe devised for converting the stone barn into a weekend hideaway across a staggered floor plan. "The spaces all connect in an open plan," says Howe. "The living room opens out directly into the wildflower meadow and in the summer the double-glass doors can be swung back to allow the ducks to waddle in, along with the odd sheep. In the winter it becomes a cozy spot with a log burner providing the extra boost of heat and atmosphere," says Howe. "There's so much to explore with the dogs; we've not even touched the surface."

ABOVE: Apollo Slimline Hipster and Great Bear peruse their many leisure options from the bench carved out of a fallen tree.

OPPOSITE: The house's four large rooms on two floors are bisected via the generous staircase. The old Victorian cast-iron newel post was the starting point for the new handrail and balustrades, which were forged by a local smithy. An abstract painting by Martin Finnin, a contemporary Irish artist, hangs on the reclaimed timber wall boards. The ample ottoman is made by HOWE.

OPPOSITE: A Jean Royère floor lamp easily mixes with a relief painting by a WWII officer, created while he was a prisoner in the 1940s.

ABOVE: Apollo Slimline Hipster keeps watch from a Made by HOWE Mark chair covered in the not-so-mud-resistant Thimble Print Linen, 'Little Weed' from 36 Bourne Street. "Most everything in the barn, especially on the ground floor, is meant to take muddy paws," says Howe. "After all, we are in the middle of a field, so you can't be too precious."

ABOVE AND FOLLOWING SPREAD: The sunken kitchen is always filled with the bounty of local produce. Howe makes daily trips to the nearby village. "I always go to see Mrs. Watkins at the local baker and grocery shop. I love talking to her—she is ninety-eight, I think—and her son Chris is the baker. You have to preorder or you won't get a loaf." The eighteenth-century Norwegian painted dresser was a lucky fit for the kitchen.

RIGHT: In the entry, coat hooks are laden with various leads for dogs of many sizes and coats and headgear for every type of weather and occasion. The primitive nineteenth-century wooden sign on the wall reads:

BE YE WUMMIN
BE YE MANNIN
BE YE CUMMIN
BE YE GANNIN
BE YE EARLY
BE YE LATE
DINNA FORGET
TO SHUT THE GATE

OPPOSITE: Everything in Howe's cottage is there for comfort or has a story to tell. "Comfort is key, I suppose," Howe says. "This is achieved by the mixture of old and new, quality and character, and perhaps most importantly by being surrounded by the things we love and find useful, just as William Morris would have said."

PAGES 82–83: In the barn's master bedroom, Howe draped a sixteenth-century English bed in a horse's linen wicking sheet— a nod to the area's strong link with horse training—and added some handmade vintage pillows. The timber-clad walls upstairs are limewashed to provide natural protection and to reflect more light from the original Serge Mouille three-armed ceiling light.

Edward Bulmer, Molly, and Lenny

DESIGNER
Edward Bulmer
Interior designer specializing in historic buildings and founder of Edward Bulmer Natural Paint

DOGS
Molly, age nine
Bedlington lurcher cross

Lenny, age two
Miniature smooth-haired dachshund

THEIR COUNTRY HOME
Court of Noke
Herefordshire, England

"MY EMPHASIS IS TO ALWAYS MAKE a house a home," says interior designer and renowned architectural historian Edward Bulmer. Bulmer trained with the well-respected designer David Mlinaric and picture restorer and designer Alec Cobbe, and this has always been his mission—whether updating Althorp, the childhood home of Diana, Princess of Wales, or creating an eponymous environmentally friendly paint collection.

But perhaps there is no better example than the redbrick Queen Anne home in the historic county of Herefordshire that he shares with his wife, Emma, and their two dogs. "Molly and Lenny had a hard act to follow after our beloved cocker spaniel Lucy passed away," says Bulmer. "My wife brought home Molly as a puppy, after my only request was that we did not get a terrier as they are impossible to house-train. Apparently, she did not realize that the Bedlington part of the mix was indeed a terrier. But Molly has been wonderful." Lenny was brought into the fold when the Bulmers' youngest daughter requested a miniature dachshund after the family had recovered from their loss of Lucy. "My youngest daughter, Kitty, rarely asks for anything, so her wish was granted," says Bulmer.

The dogs found their footing as a team and now love to meander from house to office with walks around the farm and garden once a day, including stops at a restored eighteenth-century water garden, built during the reign of William III, that weaves its way around the house. The Bulmers live in the country full-time; their office is a converted farm building next to the house. Emma co-owns and manages Edward Bulmer Natural Paint.

Brought up in a nearby Georgian rectory, Edward saw the house as a child and was enchanted with its charming facade of brick and hub of outbuildings. After their marriage, the couple discovered that the house was for sale, and it became theirs in 1994. Centuries of various stages of living and neglect had left the house in a sorry state, so the Bulmers set out to completely revamp it.

They put in a new wing to face the walled garden, enlarged the kitchen, and unblocked many windows to bring the light back in. They placed cheerful colors on the walls (from the Bulmer paint collection, naturally) and comfortable furniture (some designed by Edward) on the floors, and personal mementos on the oak-paneled walls alongside pictures by family and friends. "We have remodeled it considerably to be a warm, practical home for our three daughters, two dogs, and a cat," says Emma. The dogs have recently been allowed to curl up on the sofas, now that the last of their daughters has gone to university.

Outside, the series of four canal-like ponds, river, watermill, and old cider orchard offer endless adventures for dogs and humans alike. The Bulmers have planted allées of hornbeam and created areas of topiary to offset the canals. Lenny and Molly take regular walks around the property, with dashes into the design office to check in on things and sometimes to do a bit of gardening. "They try to help us when we dig in roses," says Edward, "though they never seem to get the holes in the right place."

The Bulmers love to entertain, and if guests bring their dogs it's even better since there is always extra room to spread a dog bed or two

in the boot room. For meals, Lenny has a labyrinthine spiral bowl "to amuse him into eating more slowly," says Edward, while Molly sups her biscuits and meat from a steel bowl. When weather permits, the dogs sleep in their handsome pedimented kennel next to the main house's coming-and-going door.

"Having dogs ensures you can't be utterly selfish," says Emma. "After all," adds Edward, "how can you have a proper country house without dogs?"

PREVIOUS SPREAD: Edward with Lenny and Molly in a room entirely of the Bulmers making. The paneling was constructed from their own oak trees and painted in the color Pomona from Edward Bulmer Natural Paint. Edward painted the views of the Taj Mahal and designed the sofa, which Emma upholstered in pink leather. David Bamford made the hand-knotted rug based on an old Bessarabian design.

LEFT: The Bulmers' brick house was built around 1700, and it enchanted Edward as a child growing up nearby. Since becoming the owners twenty-five years ago, the Bulmers have set about completely restoring it. The formal fishponds, known as canals, contemporary with the house, had all but vanished. The Bulmers are gradually reinstating them. The dogs, however, prefer paddling in the nearby River Arrow to swimming in the canals.

ABOVE: The entrance hall, painted in Lilac Pink from Edward Bulmer Natural Paint.

OPPOSITE: Molly always finds the warm floors as the sun moves around the house. She starts
her day in the eighteenth-century paneled oak room.

OPPOSITE: Lenny perches on a bench brought back from the couple's Sri Lankan honeymoon. The hand-painted wallpaper was made in China in the early nineteenth century for the European export market. Bulmer designed the bed with a custom-woven striped silk.

LEFT: In the mudroom, Molly sleeps on an oak settle carved by Emma's great-grandfather.

BELOW: Lenny and Molly have adopted the Lelièvre mohair velvet Mousse sofa, designed by Bulmer, in the house's conservatory.

ABOVE: Molly and Lenny often have their neighbor, Alf, a working cocker spaniel, over from next-door. Downtime is spent in the kennel. It was designed by Bulmer, who was inspired by Thomas Jefferson after touring Jefferson's Virginia estate, Monticello.

OPPOSITE: The Bulmers planted the arcaded hornbeam tunnel to celebrate the millennium. Dachshunds love tunneling, and Lenny is no exception.

Emma Burns
and Dahlia Mary

DESIGNER
Emma Burns
*Interior decorator
and design director
at Sibyl Colefax &
John Fowler*

DOG
Dahlia Mary, age
nineteen months
Black pug

THEIR COUNTRY HOME
*Oxfordshire Village,
England*

INTERNATIONAL INTERIOR DESIGNER Emma Burns named her black pug Dahlia Mary because for generations all the girls in Burns's family have had Mary as a second name. However, she says with a cheeky smile, "Dahlia really should be called 'White Fang,' considering how much she chews." Undaunted and besotted since day one, Burns had been patiently waiting for a year for Dahlia. "I had to prove I was a suitable candidate to her breeder, which was quite tricky given my advanced age," says Burns, who flirted with the idea of a beige rescue pug before realizing that she wanted to embrace puppyhood. "When Dahlia finally arrived at nine weeks old, she was an adorable shiny black bundle with an enormous personality from day one," says Burns. "I felt she knew immediately that I was the one for her."

Their weekdays are spent together in London's Belgravia neighborhood in Burns's bustling office where Dahlia has a built-in alarm that at 3:55 p.m. sharp reminds her, and everyone else, that she needs to sit on a lap and be hugged. "In the office we take turns cradling her at once. Dahlia likes to scheme and throw fabrics around, so it can be disruptive," says Burns. But Dahlia is not so disruptive that Burns cannot fulfill her very in-demand work around the globe as an interior designer, whether outfitting a family camp in Wisconsin, complete with twig work by local artisans framing birch paneled walls; or in Moscow, transforming a suburban villa by upholstering walls with deep bronze mohair velvets and embellishments of gilded fillets. For a plantation house in the Caribbean, "It is sophisticated simplicity of the highest order," says Burns. "We even sprayed the golf carts the same color as the turquoise sea."

Burns began at Colefax in 1984 under the tutelage of its infamous decorator Roger Banks-Pye. "He was so inspirational and so generous with his knowledge, and taught me everything I know, especially how to break the decorating rules, and how to make a room sing," says Burns.

When the weekend arrives, Burns and Dahlia hustle out of London in a car laden with the stuff that makes country houses hum. "My son and daughter are quite used to sitting in huge discomfort with a piece of furniture on their laps or among piles of old linens to be made into garden cushions," says Burns unapologetically. "Dahlia pug rides in splendor and great comfort in her crate, which takes the entirety of the boot."

Their converted eighteenth-century dovecote originally belonged to one of the big properties in the picturesque village and then later to Burns's parents, who are also pug owners. They discovered its charming yet derelict state while on a stroll, then bought the house and spent years restoring it before Burns came into it in 2002 to continue in the quest of its continual metamorphosis. "It's rare for me to arrive at the weekends without something for the house, plundered from our Pimlico showroom or stuff swapped with something from my London home. I'm constantly playing 'house' and will never stop. Dahlia thankfully supports this." Burns definitely made the dovecote's interior feel less "polite vicarage" and more glamorous, with its thunder-gray walls and Robert Kime's dramatic Opium Poppy linen slipcovers for the upholstery. The separate building just a few yards away on the property, down a flagstone path, was initially a hay barn and then "the world's biggest garden shed until I finally converted it into a library for my ever-growing collection of books," says Burns. Here, they fill the two extensive galleries, all painted tirelessly by Burns herself in Farrow & Ball's Shaded White Lime Wash and are accessed from library ladders. "Not everyone is happy to climb a ladder, it turns out.

They tend to sort the men from the boys," says Burns. Retreating here affords much time to read her beloved trove of tomes, expertly organized (Burns having been a librarian at her school at age ten) with literature A to Z, history, biography, travel, gardening, diaries, reference, poetry, and children's books, with Dahlia snuggled by her side on a wide Louis Philippe daybed tucked up next to a great Suzani on the wall. This spot handily doubles as an extra bedroom in a pinch.

In the main house's kitchen, Dahlia likes to snooze in front of the AGA stove in a wicker bed that once belonged to Maud, Burns's mother's last pug. "Dahlia has remodeled the bed, chewing off the sides and back to customize it as her own," says Burns, who softens the rough tatters with a black sheepskin or a lap rug. Dahlia does not eat in the kitchen, however, as "her table manners leave much to be desired." Burns instead leaves fresh water in a Romanian slipware bowl and food in an eco-friendly bamboo food bowl from Whole Foods outside the kitchen door. Breakfast is a four-minute soft-boiled egg, with a smattering of biscuits. Supper is at 5 p.m.—although Dahlia tries to bring it forward every day by five minutes—and often consists of raw mince. "She's not picky, just greedy beyond imagination," says Burns.

"After eating she picks a fight with her bed and tosses it around for fun." Other cherished rituals involve bounding around the house's walled garden where Dahlia is allowed to roam freely. However, inside the house there is part of an old rabbit's pen reinterpreted to keep her on the ground floor. But it is not always effective. "The telltale heavy breathing will let you know she has snuck upstairs and is lurking outside a bedroom door," says Burns. "Dahlia can cultivate a look of great innocence, which can prove irresistible." When she is not bounding and sneaking about, this pug—like so many of her breed—adores chewing. "The game of untying my laces never fails to entertain Dahlia, and I am sure sales of Converse have skyrocketed as a result of her foot obsession," says Burns. One of their favorite pastimes à deux is strolling around the village. "Often we play Poohsticks à la Christopher Robin on the little bridge over the stream behind the butcher's, knocking twigs into the water to see whose gets from one side to the other first," says Burns. "She is quite competitive."

No matter where they are walking, Burns has important advice to share. "Always carry poo bags—I once had to rip the last page from a book I was reading to scoop the poop and never found out how the story ended." Another tip: Burns recommends being prepared for the inevitable shedding. "I mostly wear blue and wanted a navy pug, but they don't make them yet." But Burns wouldn't have Dahlia any other way. "She's my demon and a great seducer of people," says Burns. "The unconditional love of a pug is worth more than all the tea in China, which is where they came from."

PREVIOUS SPREAD: Burns and Dahlia like to spend every weekend they can in the country, and are forever spiffing the place up.

LEFT: The converted eighteenth-century dovecote originally belonged to Emma Burns's parents, also pug owners, and was discovered by them while on a stroll.

ABOVE: In the entry, an eighteenth-century English long-case clock with blue lacquer and gilded decoration keeps company with a zebra skin rug, with some "chew" detailing provided by Dahlia. The old flagstone floor "perfectly caters to all eventualities," says Burns. "It's amazing for muddy boots, paws, and dripping umbrellas."

OPPOSITE: Dahlia poises halfway up the front staircase, which Burns has covered with vintage Persian runners. "They are super practical and forgiving, since they hide any muddy paw marks and black pug hairs," says Burns. The lamp is a converted nineteenth-century blue-and-white jar from Colefax & Fowler with a handmade shade in old Turkish ticking, and the bureau is a late eighteenth-century oak chest of drawers. All the woodwork is painted in Farrow & Ball Railings, and the walls are Farrow & Ball Buff.

ABOVE: In the drawing room, the sofa is covered in Robert Kime's Opium Poppy Bright. "I adore this linen, and love it against the thundery gray of the walls," says Burns. "It is a fantastic background for the old textiles that the cushions are made from. It's timeless, inviting, and smart all at once."

OPPOSITE: Each weekend, Burns brings flowers from London's flower markets. "I love to mix dahlias with the Japanese anemones I grow in the garden," says Burns.

OPPOSITE: Family paintings cozy up a wall: on top, a portrait of Burns's great grandmother, and in the middle, a picture painted by her brother of Burns's great uncle. At the bottom is a painting found at a junk shop. Burns explains that she added it because "I felt that my mother's last pug, Maud, needed an ancestor."

ABOVE: In the pantry, reclaimed doors were used for the kitchen cupboards that Burns found in a reclamation yard near Cheltenham, Gloucestershire. The nineteenth-century painted tole tray was a wedding present to her parents.

RIGHT: Dahlia pauses between adventures on her much-chewed dog bed, which has been covered with a lap rug to stop her from poking an eye out. "She sleeps like a log here, thanks to the warmth of the AGA," says Burns.

FOLLOWING SPREAD: In the kitchen the "Trays for the Sands" sign was used in a 1980s television commercial. "It fits so perfectly above the window and is deliciously enigmatic," says Burns. "None of us understand what it means." Her collection of nineteenth-century Staffordshire pottery spaniels below it has "snowballed" over the years. The traditional four-oven AGA stove in cream "is the best thing in the house, and keeps everything warm all year round," says Burns. "We never turn it off."

PAGES 106-107 The seventeenth-century elm beams, original to the house, frame the master bedroom where Dahlia finds her way onto Emma's bed, covered in an incredibly fragile antique patchwork quilt. "This is why Dahlia is not allowed up on my bed. There is less of it every time I look at it," says Burns.

ABOVE: Dahlia sports a leather collar set with malachite stones made by Claire Fouché. "It's inspired by antique dog collar curtain rings crossed with eighteenth-century Meissen porcelain pugs," says Burns. "It was given to me as a birthday present by my office and it's the most beautiful collar possible, for the most beautiful black pug imaginable."

OPPOSITE: "We delay departure for as long as possible, preferring to get up at an ungodly hour to squeeze one more walk in daylight," says Burns about the weekend's end. "Dahlia arrived here as a tiny puppy of nine weeks old, and it's in her DNA. She is her happiest here."

Gavin Houghton, Jack, and Jill

DESIGNER
Gavin Houghton
Interior designer

DOGS
Jack and Jill, both age three
Jack Russell terriers

THEIR COUNTRY HOME
Sandford St. Martin, England

FOR A LUCKY FEW, DESTINY can be found on the Internet. It was thanks to preloved.co.uk for uniting two Jack Russell terriers, Jack and Jill, with designer Gavin Houghton. "It sounded like a dating app, which it may as well have been considering how much I love them," says Houghton, joking.

The besotted trio spend every weekend they can, leaving their weekday Victorian terrace house in Stockwell for the country. "We all jump into the filthy Renault Clio with the dogs in the back on their tartan rug," says Houghton. Their destination is outside of Oxford, in a cozy retreat along a row of early Cotswold cottages. "It was probably once for the servants for the big house nearby," says Houghton, a Brit, who shares it with Boz Gagovski, an interiors photographer from Macedonia. "It is a listed village. There are no streetlamps or any modern signage, so it looks very old-fashioned, which we love, and is pitch-black at night."

When Houghton took over the house seven years ago, the walls in the sitting room were a dead salmon pink, which he decided to change to green. "I call it Kermit Green," says Houghton, who opened a bustling design business in London ten years ago, after editorial and styling stints at the *World of Interiors* and *British Vogue*. "It sounds crazy but works very well. Since I've done it, I often use the same hue for clients' homes—and everyone loves it."

Houghton brings lots of vintage Colefax & Fowler prints into his country cottage. "It is great fun decorating a weekend cottage, since it is a little like playing house and you can use things that you might chuck out in London. Every piece here is dog friendly. I'm not as strict about that as I am in London." The dogs, "who luckily have very good taste," join Houghton on regular visits to the local junk shops for paintings and china. "I religiously like to add to what I think of as my Charleston—Bloombury Group's country house—moment," says Houghton. "Love a plate on the wall."

During evenings friends from neighboring villages come over for supper in the cozy kitchen. "I can literally open the oven from my seat," says Houghton. Homemade comfort food like chicken pie peppered with lardons, leeks, and tarragon is served accompanied by "buckets of red wine."

The dogs sleep together on a big tweed dog bed, inherited from a friend who lost his two elderly pugs, in front of the fire in the sitting room. "In the mornings they race up to our room for a snog, get under the covers, and then we all sleep some more," says Houghton. "Also, we love to watch crap TV in a huge pile on bad weather days."

But it is not all about reposing. Walks are a crucial part of their country days, through the village and often beyond, as is fetching sticks. "Jack and Jill were originally brought up in the city of Bradford, so the country is magical for them," says Houghton. "They nearly caught a pheasant the first time I took them out."

PREVIOUS SPREAD: Jack and Houghton seated in front of a stretched canvas hinged screen Houghton painted after studying fashion at Kingston Polytechnic. Jill eagerly looks on. The silver leaf shade was gilded for a client who did not like it, so Houghton stuck the trim on and kept it.

OPPOSITE: In the cottage's kitchen, Houghton hung a fall-and-rise lantern from HOWE London above the table. The green plates are from a junk shop in Chipping Norton. Houghton bought a huge pile of them since they complement the sitting room walls.

ABOVE: "I'm known for enjoying green in my work, so when I took the cottage, I wanted to put my stamp on it," says Houghton. "This room was painted a dead salmon color that didn't resonate with me, so I chose what I now like to refer to as 'Kermit Green.'" The painted border is by Houghton, who was inspired by Charleston in East Sussex, a farmhouse where the Bloomsbury Group, a group of artists and intellectuals, once lived.

FOLLOWING SPREAD: The terriers hang out on their favorite spot in the master bedroom. The bedcover is an Indian block print that Houghton bought in Delhi, and the pillows are from Robert Kime. "The dogs love to run upstairs after breakfast and go right under the covers," says Houghton.

ABOVE: Jill keeping watch from the master bedroom out to the garden.

OPPOSITE: Houghton and the dogs take morning coffee in the little patio garden. The café table and chairs are vintage.

FOLLOWING SPREAD: Jack and Jill love to drag Houghton through their quaint little village of Sandford St. Martin. "Once I adopted them from an urban life in North England, they adapted to country life in minutes," says Houghton.

Justin Van Breda, Margot, and Maudie

DESIGNER
Justin Van Breda
*Interior designer and
furniture designer*

DOGS
Margot, age ten
Labrador Retriever

Maudie, age five
Labrador Retriever

THEIR COUNTRY HOME
Gloucestershire, England

"WE EITHER HAVE NOTHING TOO precious or we are not too precious about anything," says Justin Van Breda about sharing country life in the Cotswolds with his partner, Alastair Matchett, and their two yellow labs, Margot and Maudie. Margot was a surprise gift from Van Breda for Matchett's fortieth birthday. "She was so tiny at six weeks, and I carried her into the drawing room with a red bow around her neck," says Van Breda. "And Maudie we bred from Margot. She was the runt of the litter of eight puppies and is deaf. But because Maudie lives with her mother, she follows her lead and is fiercely independent. And as she was born in the house, she is very entitled."

Weekend life revolves around their Georgian stone house, built in 1792 and completed in 1840. History runs deep here both outside and within. A folly in the garden was built to display Roman finds from a nearby archaeological site, some of which are now in the British Museum. The kitchen includes the original cider press. "The house is restored and decorated in a mix of styles. I am not too much of a purist," says Van Breda, who was born in South Africa. "We'll have some Ardmore ceramics from Africa on a George I table or use a contemporary table as a base for an heirloom eighteenth-century Chinese fisherman sculpture."

Van Breda opened his London design firm in 2002. The dogs travel with him to his showroom and studio in Chelsea during the busy weekdays and sleep under his desk. His furniture collection, which is handmade in Europe, was inspired by the house's heritage. Come Friday when they arrive in the country, the dogs love to bound around the garden areas, including the large rose garden, planted with the roses Van Breda and Matchett received as gifts for their civil partnership. The roses cover the color spectrum, from 'Winchester Cathedral' white to 'Gertrude Jekyll' magenta. The dogs also enjoy the barn garden of flowering grasses and box hedging and an orchard planted with trees bestowed on Matchett as a birthday gift by friends. "Gardening is a big part of our lives," says Van Breda. "While we do it, the dogs lie on the lawn and look at us curiously."

At night, they sometimes dine at local restaurants that welcome dogs or entertain at home. The frequent guests are Margot's puppies, one who went to a friend in London and another to a family of god-children in West Sussex. "Being the alpha, Margot is very calm when people and other dogs visit. Maudie generally goes hysterical and then calms down," says Van Breda.

Often on the menu is old-fashioned roast chicken or deboned leg of lamb, with the raw bones saved for the dogs, and Van Breda's grandmother's apple crumble for dessert. The dogs enjoy a raw food diet prepared by Honey's Real Dog Food from white and blue-rimmed enamel mixing bowls, which were inspired by the dog bowls at the kennels at Goodwood in Chichester.

When it is time for bed, Margot and Maudie sleep in the master bedroom in woven baskets that Van Breda bought from the Cape Town Society for the Blind. In the morning as a treat, they are allowed on the bed before another productive yet restorative day begins. One thing that is a constant is Van Breda's unwavering commitment to his family being together. "The dogs are a huge part of our world, and my conscious daily routine revolves around them."

PREVIOUS SPREAD: Van Breda stands just outside the kitchen with Margot at his knee and Maudie close by. The climbing rose is 'Teasing Georgia.' The house is built from Cotswold stone.

RIGHT: Followed by Margot, Van Breda walks next to the orchard below the house, which is planted with an assortment of fruit trees. The house was built from 1792 to 1840, and its exterior has remained unchanged since.

OPPOSITE: Van Breda sits on the bleached iroko wood surface of the custom kitchen cabinets with Margot nearby on the English stone floor. The walls are painted Farrow & Ball Slipper Satin, and the cabinetry is in their Shaded White. The fireplace surround is original to the house and its finish is exactly as it was found by Van Breda's partner, Alastair Matchett, when they bought the house over twenty years ago.

ABOVE: The dresser is original to the house, and its scalloped shelving can be seen in some of the built-in joinery. It holds Van Breda's collection of creamware, silver jugs, and teapots, which are used every day.

FOLLOWING SPREAD: The dining room wall is covered in a custom print of John Constable's *Wivenhoe Park* (1816), which hangs in the National Gallery in Washington, DC. It was printed on linen canvas by Van Breda. The chairs, table, and sideboard are all from Van Breda's English Home Furniture Collection. The tree branch mobile from which glass candle globes hang came from the garden. "I wanted the whole room to make you feel as if you were sitting in a park looking at the house," says Van Breda.

The George III mahogany table that came from Van Breda's father stands in the Georgian window
of the drawing room and shows off some of Matchett's collections of bronze Grand Tour and
dog sculptures. The Augustus armchair from Van Breda's furniture line is covered in Trailing Hawthorne
from his English Fabric Collection. The 'Queen of the Night' tulips come from the garden.

Margot and Maudie sleep in the master bedroom in a basket woven by the blind in South Africa with whom Van Breda produces a collection of furniture. The antique furniture consists of family pieces. The fabric on the headboard is from Colefax & Fowler, and the linen on the chairs is Brighton Beach from Van Breda's English Fabric Collection.

ABOVE: Maudie's Union Jack collar was hand-beaded in Kenya.

OPPOSITE: Both Margot and Maudie follow Van Breda into the walled garden that flanks the house from the paddock that surrounds the property. The huge yew tree that casts valuable shade is about two hundred years old.

Katharine Pooley and Herbie Bullet Voyce

DESIGNER
Katharine Pooley
*Interior designer
and author*

DOG
Herbie Bullet Voyce,
age six months
Jack Russell terrier

THEIR COUNTRY HOME
The Coach House
Oxfordshire, England

"OUR NEW DOG HAD big paws to fill," says Katharine Pooley. She had recently lost her beloved Piglet, a Jack Russell terrier who lived with her in Hong Kong, Singapore, and then London, until he passed away at the age of eighteen. It turns out that young Herbie, also a Jack Russell, is the perfect combination of gentle temperament and boisterous character. "Having a dog is all about an adventure no matter where you are," says Pooley. And she should know, having visited over 150 countries, summited many of the world's highest mountains, driven a team of dogs to the North Pole, ridden horseback across the Sahara, and even trekked to see gorillas in Virunga, Rwanda.

But there is also plenty for her and Herbie to explore right at home at The Coach House, the weekend refuge they share with Pooley's husband, Dan, and their two boys, Jack and Charlie. "The Coach House is very much a home within the great outdoors, so there are endless excursions for Herbie among the fields and wildlife," says Pooley. Set within an estate of mature trees and parkland, the house has been renovated and fashioned into an elegant and calm oasis. Its site dates back to an eighth-century estate. "This is where I come to wind down and do all the things I love with my family, so the interior had to have a sophistication, but it also has to be home for my boys and dog." She mixed modern pieces with antiques and bespoke fabrics and used serene colors for the walls, such as aqua and creamy grays. The rooms are open and encourage conversation and play, be it on two legs or four. In the kitchen, Pooley loves to cook worldly dishes like slow-roasted lamb with pomegranate—she graduated from the Cordon Bleu cooking school and has written a cookbook. Herbie can be found close by in his dog bed where the radio is often tuned to a classical station to keep him company at night. Another favorite spot is the horse box library, a reading haven for the boys. "We wanted to give it the feel of a fun outdoor library but keep it child's scale," says Pooley, who lined the freestanding structure's back window with tiny curtains bound with leather to create a shelved sanctuary based on old-fashioned mobile libraries.

Nearby is another separate, albeit more grown-up and stylish destination to visit: the custom shepard's hut. By thoughtfully outfitting the tiny space with antiques, a tented ceiling, a bespoke bed, sisal carpeting, and a woodburning stove, Pooley created a gypsy caravan suitable for a stylish country squire. Along the six acres of the estate's grounds, she has cultivated a garden with raised beds so Herbie can't squash the seedlings and a brimming vegetable patch. Herbie accompanies her for the daily collection of eggs from the chicken hut, which protects the four resident chickens from foxes. Pooley had a Hamptons architect fashion it from online plans.

"Whatever the task here, it is the ideal break from the bustle of our London life," says Pooley, who oversees forty-five interior designers at her busy firm. They help her realize projects around the world, whether a beach house in Cape Town or a palace in Kuwait. "When I need to travel back to my Knightsbridge office, Herbie often comes with me. He is very much at home in the design studio there and a great addition to the team, not to mention my family. I love having a shadow again—the house and family are a different place having him in our world."

133

PREVIOUS SPREAD: Pooley standing with Herbie on the front steps of The Coach House, flanked by a pair of dog sculptures, beneath the elegant sandstone Georgian arched facade.

ABOVE: Pooley spent many years living in Asia and this influence is apparent in her eclectic and luxurious design style. In this corner of her living room, a blue and gold chinoiserie cabinet sits beside a pair of blue-and-white ginger jars.

OPPOSITE: At the expansive antique mahogany dining table, Herbie helps Pooley address client projects worldwide. The gold Buddhas are from Pooley's Knightsbridge boutique.

OPPOSITE: Herbie likes to relax on cushions on the lawn beside Pooley's vegetable patch in the sunshine, the perfect spot to keep an eye out for rabbits. The cushion on the right is covered in Katie Ridder's Pagoda Elephant pattern.

ABOVE: In a quiet corner of the coach house's surrounding parkland, under the dappled light from an oak tree, Pooley's previous and much-loved dogs have a final resting place.

RIGHT: Pooley's son Jack, resplendent in a kilt, hugs best friend Herbie on the ramp to the horse box library snug, a converted horse box that is the perfect spot for whiling away a rainy afternoon.

BELOW: Pooley's lifelong love for dogs is alluded to in her car's personalized number.

OPPOSITE: Pooley's sons, Jack and Charlie, peek out with Herbie from the doorway to the shepard's hut. Originally created by Pooley to be a luxurious outside guest bedroom overlooking the grounds, it is now often commandeered by the boys for "war games" with Herbie.

Kit Kemp, Impy, Paddington, Button, Rupert, and Pixie

DESIGNER
Kit Kemp
*Interior designer,
creative director of
Firmdale Hotels
and textile and
homewares designer*

DOGS
Impy, age thirteen
*Cavalier King
Charles spaniel*

Paddington, age thirteen
*Cavalier King
Charles spaniel*

Button, age seven
*Cavalier King
Charles spaniel*

Rupert, age three
*Cavalier King
Charles spaniel*

Pixie, age three
*Cavalier King
Charles spaniel*

THEIR COUNTRY HOME
New Forest, England

IT IS COMMON TO SEE SEVERAL GENERATIONS of a human family take a dog or two on an excursion to the country. But in the case of the Kemps, it is three generations of dogs who accompany Kit and her husband Tim from their London town house to their weekend home every weekend and holiday. The five Cavalier King Charles spaniels are from the same family line. Impy and Paddington are siblings, Impy is Button's mother, and Button is Rupert and Pixie's mother. They ride three in the back seat on a blanket and two in the front, with Rupert between the driver and the passenger seats so he can help with the navigation. "When you have one dog, you suddenly seem to have five," says Kemp, who switches to a "dog car" once they get to the country, which usually stays very muddy. "But there's something incredibly special about having an extended family within our own."

Once they reach their destination in scenic New Forest, there are both woodlands and the sea to entice every kind of canine caper. A nineteenth-century cottage sitting on four acres is home base. Kemp, who grew up in the area, found the house over twenty years ago after renting a cottage nearby. Determined to bring her effervescent and elegant style to the retreat's interiors much in the way she designed all ten of her celebrated Firmdale Hotels, which she co-owns with Tim, Kemp crafted every room to feel like it belongs to a unique person rather than to a brand. "I don't think homes should be too tailored," says Kemp, who also designs textiles, fragrances, and housewares. "A home should tell a story about who lives there, and that is what ours is like." Kemp tells her "perfectly imperfect" story with an inventive take on fabrics, such as using ribbed pink corduroy with blue piping or finishing bright floral printed curtains and cushions with pearlized shell trim. Kemp also delights with twists on other unexpected details, such as draping driftwood on an old horse head door knocker or perching the scull of an old boat between some ceiling beams. They are all woven into the traditional hallmarks of a country home—such as an old writing desk, vintage ceramics, and raised fireplaces where the dogs love to curl up *en famille*.

Outside, Kemp commissioned stone sculptor Tom Stogdon to create a large slate circle to sit in a garden, sublimely framing the Beaulieu River in the distance. "I like to have destinations throughout the property to encourage people to go out and explore, and the dogs love to join them," says Kemp. "They'll even jump through the sculpture on their way to catch a ball. But Impy does not allow the other dogs to return it unless she grabs hold of their ear and pulls them."

Sundays are special, because some of Button's puppies, who now live in friends' homes, often come to visit. Parents and their pups congregate in the large kitchen with its AGA stove. "There can be seven or eight dogs sitting in a semicircle around Tim, watching him carve the meat and waiting for a bit of roast to fall on the floor," says Kemp.

"Ours is a really open house to everyone who crosses its threshold, be they on two or four legs." After the guests have departed, the dogs sleep in the utility room beneath baskets reserved for the cats Kipper, a tabby, and Raddish, who is all white.

Kemp's collection of dog paintings can be seen throughout the house, some she found while traveling and others were painted by her daughter Willow, who works on Kemp's design team, along with her sister Araminta, who goes by "Min." (Kemp's other daughter, Tiffany, lives near the country house and works for Oxfam and also volunteers with disabled adults.) No matter the origin of the paintings, they remind Kit of the antics and expressions of her actual pets. "My dogs have always made me laugh."

PREVIOUS SPREAD: In the master bedroom, Kit Kemp made the bed around the fluted carved wooden bedposts with a ribbon carved in wood around their length. The fabric is a copy of Maria Sibylla's botanical drawing produced by Chelsea Textiles. "I love the vibrant colors and the scale of it," says Kemp. The sofa is covered in Kit Kemp's Friendly Folk pattern in Huntsman Red.

RIGHT: Kemp sits with the dogs in front of a Tom Stogdon stone circle in the garden. The main part of the house is early twentieth century, made of local Beaulieu brick, which has a smaller gauge than normal bricks. The window surrounds are of solid oak.

BELOW: The dogs wait by the front door hoping for an afternoon walk before tea. The clock is an heirloom from Kemp's parents' house.

RIGHT: Rupert and Pixie asleep on one of the pink velvet sofas in the wood room. "Pink transforms a serious room into a space that feels so happy and welcoming," says Kemp. The inglenook fireplace makes this a cozy room on winter evenings.

FOLLOWING SPREAD: Impy, Rupert, Button, Pixie, and Paddy sit on the sofa as Kipper the cat elegantly watches from her cardboard cat theater, which was made by a friend of Kemp's who is based in Biarritz. The cushions are designed by Kemp for Fine Cell Work.

ABOVE: Old French bentwood chairs painted green sit outside Kemp's shepherd's hut on wheels. This is an ideal sheltered spot for morning coffee and birdwatching.

OPPOSITE: Impy, Pixie, and Rupert in the shepherd's hut at the bottom of the garden where Kemp goes for a bit of peace and quiet. Every square inch is patterned and painted. The sofa pattern is Friendly Folk in Basil Green from Kemp's own collection. The rabbit cushions are a prototype design for Fine Cell Work, a charity that makes handmade products in British prisons. The rug is a vintage needlepoint by Vaughan.

FOLLOWING SPREAD: Button, Rupert, and Paddy dashing in and out of the topiary creatures Kemp created, with the river in the distance.

Max Rollitt, Beano, and Ginny

DESIGNER
Max Rollitt
Antiques dealer, interior designer, furniture maker

DOGS
Beano, age nine
Parsons Russell terrier

Virginia Plain (Ginny),
age six
English pointer

THEIR COUNTRY HOME
Hampshire, England

"BEANO AND GINNY ARE the yin and yang of our household," says Max Rollitt of the Hampshire home he shares with them, along with his wife, Jane, and their four sons. "Ginny has such an enthusiasm for life, while Beano embraces an independent and adventurous spirit."

At their restored brick and flint farmhouse (the original structure built on the site of what was a priory before the Norman Conquest in 1066), Ginny enjoys following the precise trajectory of sticks and chasing after them ("We think she has studied trigonometry," says Rollitt), while Beano takes himself for a walk when the mood strikes. "Beano has apparently been employed by the local council as a traffic calming officer and can often be found on the quiet country lane near our house, observing the infrequent traffic."

The Rollitts bought the cottage and the surrounding land from a local farmer and moved there in the early 2000s. They made a decision not to change the layout and to respect the house's history despite thorough renovations. "It seems that whoever built the house made use of the materials left from the priory's demolition, as we have Gothic wooden beams, gargoyles adorn the western facade, and there is even a medieval corbel figure supporting the ceiling in the kitchen," says Rollitt, who has casually yet carefully filled the rooms with antiques culled from years of collecting, or with ones handed down through his and his wife's families.

Rollitt has a special affinity for rejuvenating materials and understanding their history. As a young man, he educated himself through courses in furniture design and cabinetmaking and then began as an apprentice, then journeyman cabinetmaker and furniture restorer before launching his own antiques business. This soon led to interior design commissions and producing his own bespoke range of furniture using traditional methods and materials. A former grain store on the property is now his showroom and design office. Beano and Ginny are occasional visitors to the office.

The scenic River Itchen runs past the house, and eventually to the sea, and the dogs have a daily walk along the riverbank, with Beano taking a swim in warm weather. Ginny prefers swimming in the sea at the Rollitts' Regency fisherman's cottage in southern Cornwall. Well-earned snoozes are next to the AGA in the kitchen, which is decorated with simple wooden furniture, including a Windsor bench designed by Rollitt.

At night, the Rollitts will often awake to find that Beano has crept upstairs to sneak into their bed. "My tip regarding dogs is make sure to train them from an early age," says Rollitt. "Beano has calmed down a lot in his middle age, but as a young Jack Russell with a mind of his own he caused us many angst-filled hours."

The Rollitts frequently entertain and encourage guests to bring their dogs. Beano and Ginny love to meet guests, as does the cat, Sushi, and pigs Betsy and Madame Whiteboots. "In general, our animals tend to rub along quite well," says Rollitt of the motley mix. "Beano is tolerated by Ginny, the pigs are tolerated by Beano, Ginny's fascinated by the chickens, and it goes without saying that Sushi the cat reigns supreme."

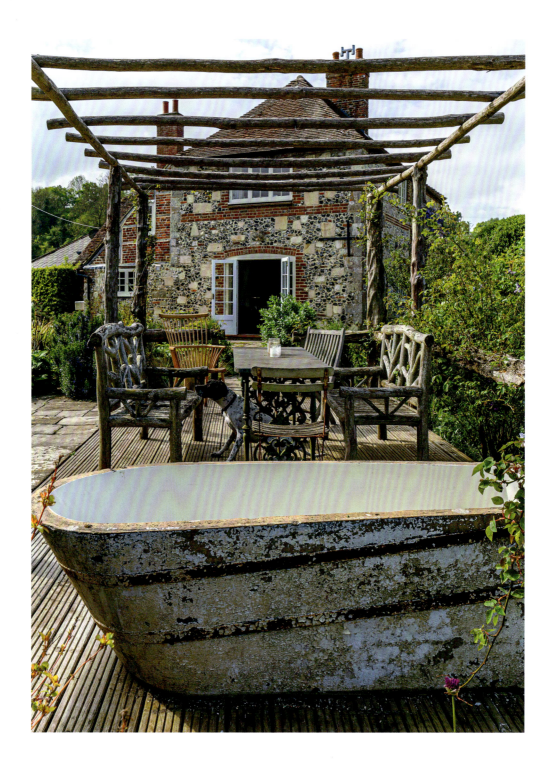

PREVIOUS SPREAD: Ginny and Rollitt in the drawing room. The whale carving, sofa, and chairs were designed by Rollitt. The Eiffel Tower drawing was done by Max's son Laurie Rollitt when he was twelve. He is now thirty-one and a professional illustrator.

ABOVE: The garden pergola was built by Rollitt for family meals and parties. There is an outside bathtub where Max and Jane can enjoy a soak under the stars.

OPPOSITE: The house, formerly part of the Avington Park estate owned by the Duke of Chandos, is very hard to date. It incorporates many building materials recovered from a twelfth-century priory that fell into ruin after the dissolution of the monasteries by Henry VIII. The coin stones are from Caen in northern France. In the roof are ancient Gothic oak beams, and within the flint walls to the sides are gargoyles. The front of the house was remodeled in the late eighteenth century.

ABOVE: A view from the hallway, with walls adorned with hats, to the music room. The curtain
is made from a beautiful piece of French bourette.

OPPOSITE: Ginny and Bcano lead Rollitt up the backstairs of his showroom in the country, past some
of his revolving collection of antiques, pictures, and signs.

ABOVE: Ginny sits with Rollitt in the music room on her favorite chair covered in a Le Manach print, which is opposite Rollitt's preferred Windsor armchair. The late seventeenth-century lacquer escritoire was purchased by Rollitt many years ago from his dear friend and fellow dealer and decorator, Edward Hurst.

RIGHT: Beano's Howard–style chair was made a long time ago by Rollitt. It has a cushion embroidered with a puppy. Above it, Rollitt's favorite vegetable, potato, is whimsically captured in a charming painting by friend Mimi Roberts.

OPPOSITE: Beano in the sunshine, waiting impatiently for his morning walk. The wallpaper is from Liberty London.

FOLLOWING SPREAD: Ginny and Beano walking home with Max and Jane on Lovington Lane. The lane divides home from work on the property. Opposite the house, Jane has her movement therapy studio, and Max has his showroom and office.

Paolo Moschino, Philip Vergeylen, and Jack

DESIGNERS
Paolo Moschino and
Philip Vergeylen
Interior designers

DOG
Jack, age one
French bulldog

THEIR COUNTRY HOME
*West Sussex, South
East England*

"WE BOUGHT THE HOUSE FROM the gate," says Philip Vergeylen of the half-Tudor, half-nineteenth-century Sussex farmhouse he shares with his partner, Paolo Moschino, and their young bulldog, Jack. "The agent was late, and we liked the look and the location of the house. We knew we would change the interior completely anyway."

There is little this formidable design duo cannot do. Moschino, who was born and raised in Italy, took over the internationally acclaimed Nicholas Haslam Ltd. twenty-five years ago and sells its furniture, fabrics, lighting collections, and antiques just off London's Pimlico Road. Eventually he started taking on interior design work for clients as well. Now Vergeylen, who was born and raised in Belgium, heads the design studio and manages projects all over the world.

Whether Vergeylen is flying to Scotland one day for a hunting lodge installation or to a ski chalet in Gstaad the next, for the past seven years he has joined Moschino and now Jack in the country where they have fashioned a retreat that feels both worldly and cozy. "The decoration of a Tudor house definitely brought some challenges," says Moschino. "There was not one straight wall or ceiling." After purchasing the house, they set about undauntedly to create smart and stylish solutions. When upholstering a wonky wall proved impossible given all the crooked beams, a trusted artisan—whose mother coincidentally lives in a Georgian rectory ten minutes away—hand-painted flowers, including the same wisteria found on the Edmond Petit textile on the bed there instead. When floors did not prove level, least-loved books were propped under bed legs to make them even. A dependable constant, however—the smooth, reclaimed Belgian oak flooring underfoot—was laid down throughout the house.

There is an abundance of beautiful objects, displayed to be intimately appreciated, whether a seventeenth-century Flemish tapestry hung to greet visitors in the entry hall, an eighteenth-century blue-and-white French painted screen mounted on the wall of the dining room, or the nineteenth-century French bed in a guest room. "We found it in a Paris flea market," says Moschino. "And once we noticed the initials 'PM' were carved on the headboard, we knew we had to bring it home."

Home is also the place where their most important treasure resides—Jack. "We have a long-standing relationship with French bulldogs, and Jack is our fifth," says Vergeylen. "We love their strong faces." Their day together starts with an early morning shared brioche, followed by exercise. Jack prefers to play within the bounds of the property and chase away pheasants.

As expert as they are at creating livable spaces, the outside grounds initially proved challenging. "When we bought the house, the garden was nothing special," says Moschino. "We are used to designing rooms

Continued on page 168

that have walls, so in the beginning we found it a bit daunting knowing where to start." Then a friend printed a Google map of the house that created a eureka moment for Vergeylen. He saw how to divide the land into six "rooms" and created six different gardens adjacent to each room, including two parterres, a pool garden, a cloud garden, a flower garden, and a wild garden.

In the winter, the house is accessed via a short train ride from London, and the trio never misses a nap together on the Belgian brushed-linen sofa after lunch in front of the fire in the drawing room. In summer months, they opt to drive to the country instead, and there, Jack takes shade under one of the sun beds by the pool. Official snoozing at night finds Jack snuggled on Porthault sheets embroidered in a rich chocolate brown chinoiserie style that complements his coloring. "Our dogs have always been allowed on all our furniture, whether here or in our London apartment, and I am happy to change the sofa slipcovers and see Jack sleeping on them," says Vergeylen.

The only challenges they have faced with dove-tailing dogs into their lives are when they are puppies. "Our dogs have always seemed to have a preference for chewing the legs of eighteenth-century bergères rather than chew toys," says Moschino, who then sprays the legs of the furniture with Tabasco sauce as a preventive measure. "It's not worth worrying about the small stuff," says Vergeylen. "After Paolo, Jack is the most important person in my life. He brings joy and total unconditional love. For us, dogs have always been a critical, essential, and most rewarding part of our lives."

PAGE 162: Moschino and Jack in their barn that has been converted into a guest wing.

PAGE 164: Vergeylen and Jack pause in the entry in front of a seventeenth-century Flemish tapestry that hangs behind a chest. A pair of Belgian lamps, made from cast-iron balusters, flanks the terra-cotta bust of Madame du Barry on top.

PAGE 165: Jack reposes in the iconic dining room that took its style cues from an eighteenth-century painted French screen, which hangs on one wall. To balance the screen with the blue-and-white china displayed on the other wall, a blossoming tree was hand-painted by Dawn Reader on the wall and the brackets.

PREVIOUS SPREAD (PAGES 166–167): The china displayed on the dining room wall is seventeenth- and eighteenth-century delft. "Most of our china—my addiction—in the country is blue-and-white," says Vergeylen. "From Meissen to Tournai, Paolo and I have about twenty-five sets. People could stay in our house for a month and never eat off of the same plate."

RIGHT: The couple wanted to have a country-style kitchen but at the same time nothing too traditional. So they opted for a gray white paint and Carrara marble.

OPPOSITE: In the dining area open to the kitchen, Jack basks in the country sunshine. "We love this room because we can enjoy the garden even when it is cold outside," says Moschino. The Belgian linen slipcovers give an intended casual look and are washable.

ABOVE, LEFT: Jack reposes on a San Patrigniano cashmere blanket in the Tudor Sussex barn's guest house.

ABOVE, RIGHT: In the living room a collection of treasures, all gifts from Vergeylen's sister Patricia.

RIGHT: In the drawing room, topiaries keep a nineteenth-century plaster cast company. Bennison's Banyan fabric covers a pillow cushion.

Moschino and Vergeylen decorated each of their five guest rooms differently. "The idea was that each time you come to stay with us you would have a different experience," says Vergeylen. "However, many of our closest friends have taken ownership of a bedroom and refuse to stay anywhere but 'their bedroom.'"

ABOVE: In the master bedroom, Jack snuggles among embroidered Porthault sheets.

OPPOSITE: Edmond Petit fabric on the headboard gives a lush, almost tropical tranquility.

OPPOSITE: The plinth was originally intended to hold a seventeenth-century Italian bust they bought from a dealer outside Florence, but Moschino and Vergeylen much preferred this owl they spotted in a window on Pimlico Road. They swapped it in instead.

ABOVE: "Years ago Paolo and I were driving around Tuscany when we passed by a field littered with reclaimed architectural elements and bought this eighteenth-century wall fountain," says Vergeylen. "We knew we had the perfect spot for it back home."

Penny Morrison, Petal, Abbi and Gobi

DESIGNER
Penny Morrison
Interior designer

DOGS
Petal, age fourteen
Jack Russell terrier

Abbi, age six
Black Labrador Retriever

Gobi, age three
Yellow Labrador Retriever

THEIR COUNTRY HOME
Wales

THREE DAYS A WEEK, PETAL, a spritely Jack Russell terrier, keeps Penny Morrison company in London at Morrison's bustling design shop. Originally from South Africa, Morrison settled in London in 1976. "I did not want to live a restricted suburban life in South Africa," says Morrison. "After a childhood spent reading Enid Blyton and other British boarding school books, I had a longing to be in England."

As soon as they are able to escape for the weekend, Petal, Penny, and her husband, fine arts dealer Guy Morrison, head to Wales to their retreat, an eighteenth-century Regency-style house, complete with Welsh-slate roofs, which Penny has lovingly restored over the past thirty years.

"When we bought the house, it had not been modernized since 1910, so it took a year of basic building work," says Morrison. "This was not helped by the fact that at the time I was pregnant and bedridden, so Guy, who had no experience in this field, had to manage the building project solo." One of the many things the Morrisons did was to line the luxurious driveway with boxwood. Since the labs prefer to stay in the country full time, they love to await Petal and Morrison's arrival at the end of the driveway.

Once reunited, the dogs enjoy diving into the ponds and exploring the woodlands that the 150-acre property affords. The Morrisons have thoughtfully carved out walks on their property that they like to roam with the dogs, as well as a pool, tennis court, and flower and vegetable gardens. "There's nothing more satisfying than walking up to the gardens on a summer's evening, selecting what looks best, and then deciding what to cook for dinner," says Morrison, who can see the border between England and Wales while she cuts a floral arrangement to dress up the dinner table.

Inside the home, Morrison's celebrated skill as both a textile and interior designer abounds, from covering the drawing room ottoman with an antique Turkish Suzani, framing the windows with curtains composed of two Claremont taffetas sewn into stripes, to slipcovering her dining room chairs in pale linen. In fact, Morrison was inspired to create her own range of elegant relaxed linen fabrics nine years ago when she had trouble finding curtain and upholstery designs that she really liked.

Entering through the front or back door, two of the house's thirteen ground-floor doors, visitors pass through curtains made from Morrison's Vilas pattern, a stylish yet relaxed portal to rooms that feel both worldly and familiar, as spirited and fresh as the Farrow & Ball Arsenic green color Morrison painted on the library walls. In the library, the three dogs love to repose in their favorite spots. Abbi and Gobi usually sit on the two red-striped armchairs with Petal favoring Morrison's lap. At night, the dogs sleep with the Morrisons on the master bed covered with a blanket. So does the resident house cat, Pluto, who sleeps on a corner of the bed.

At mealtime, Petal enjoys her food separately from the two labs in the laundry room as "she is a slower eater and the labs would scoff her food if she did not have her own space," says Morrison. Throughout the day, china bowls filled with water offer the dogs refreshment around the house.

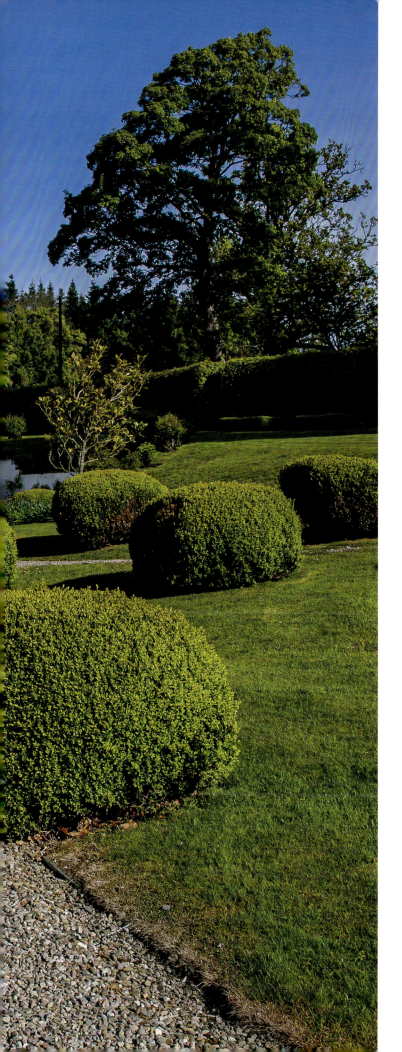

As center stage as the dogs are, they reluctantly cede the spotlight to a cockerel who comes to the front door when it gets dark, hops onto one of the sofas, and crows loudly. A flock of fifteen guinea fowl also come by and tap on the library window when they want to be fed. But, of course, it is the dogs who have Morrison's heart. "I couldn't live without dogs and we are always heartbroken when one of them dies," she says. "We have a selection of gravestones dotting the garden where previous beloved pets have been buried, along the walkways, so we can always remember them."

PREVIOUS SPREAD: Morrison in a favorite spot by the library fire, patting Abbi, who is always at her feet. The walls are painted in Farrow & Ball's Arsenic.

LEFT: Morrison and her devoted pack walk toward home along the driveway lined with boxwood balls she planted over twenty-five years ago.

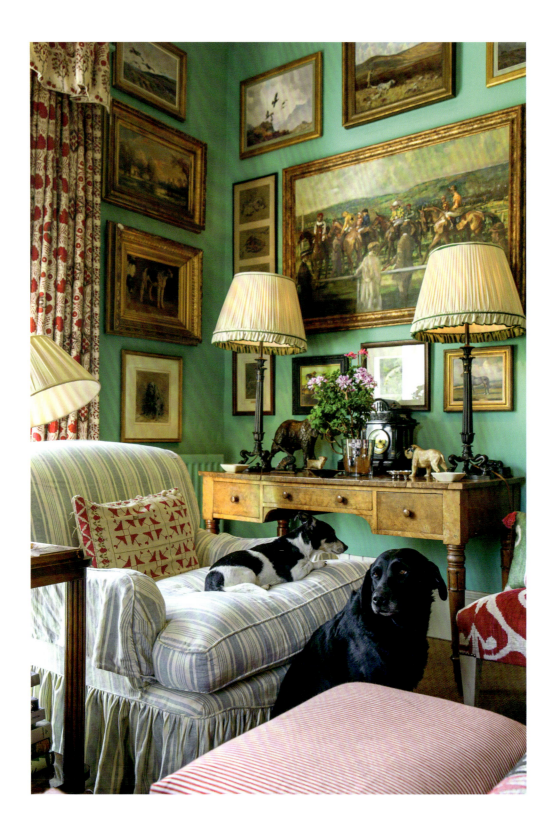

ABOVE: Abbi guards Petal, who relaxes on Morrison's husband Guy's chair in the library with the burr elm desk in the background. A painting by Tod Ramos of Cheltenham hangs above the desk.

OPPOSITE: Gobi, Abbi, and Petal wait for a treat in the front hall with Morrison's favorite view looking onto the terrace where she and the dogs congregate in summer. The rug was purchased on a trip to Marrakesh, and the lampshades are from Penny Morrison's design shop. The resplendent spray of flowers is from the cutting garden.

FOLLOWING SPREAD: The drawing room is painted in a watered-down Setting Plaster by Farrow & Ball. The portrait to the right of the fireplace is of Mrs. Edith Currie and her children, painted by Robert Brough in 1902. The portrait of the elegant lady to the left, Mrs. George Butler, was painted by Ambrose McEvoy in 1915. A favorite old Suzani is draped over the ottoman. The sofas are in a Mrs. Monro chintz.

ABOVE: Sunlight streams through one of the newly decorated guest bathrooms upstairs, covered in Aspa wallpaper by Penny's daughter, Sarah Vanrenen.

OPPOSITE: A sunny corner in the dining room. The pelmets were the only thing left by the previous owners. The striped chintz fabric used for the curtains is discontinued and the rug is a Penny Morrison design.

FOLLOWING SPREAD: In a spare bedroom, known as "Sarah's Room" (named from when Morrison's daughter was young), Gobi sits proudly on a chair covered in Roses and Pansies by Colefax and Fowler. The wallpaper is Berkeley Sprig from Colefax & Fowler, and the headboard is in their classic Bowood pattern. The rug is a needlepoint from Vaughan Designs, and the Suzani throw is from Penny Morrison's shop.

Sophie Conran and Mouse

DESIGNER
Sophie Conran
*Designer and
cookery author*

DOG
Mouse, age four
Lurcher

THEIR COUNTRY HOME
Wiltshire, England

"MOUSE IS TRULY THE LADY of the manor," says Sophie Conran of her lurcher. "She does not love London life and much prefers the open fires and the rolling downs a country house provides." For the past five years, a Georgian manor has been a resplendent abode for both dog and her human family. "It is a large, gold box full of symmetry, with incredible architecture and a bow frontage," says Conran. "It is made of Bath stone, so it has a nice soft honey color." She and Mouse share it with Conran's husband, Nick Hofgren, and children Felix and Coco. "When I bought it, I was looking for a project and this definitely is," says Conran. "We have uncovered asbestos and rotten supporting beams, but also an incredible stone staircase and original Georgian ironwork. The hard work has been more than worth it."

But no undertaking seems too formidable for Conran. In her youth, she excelled at various stylish stints: as apprentice for couture milliner Stephen Jones; assistant to her brother, fashion designer Jasper Conran; dresser of her father Sir Terence Conran's UK restaurants; and even maker of handmade lollipops. Her adult design life bursts with creativity, from authoring cookbooks to designing wallpaper, cutlery, and garden tools.

When she is not spearheading her London interior design business and online home accessories shop, Conran joins Mouse in the country four days a week. Mouse lives full time in Wiltshire and is cared for by devoted housekeepers whenever Conran is away. Once together, they roam the surrounding countryside punctuated with Iron Age hill forts, Roman roads, and neolithic standing stones. "Mouse always stays close by my side, as if she is worried that I am going to wander off," says Conran. "She is incredibly fast and loves to jump about."

In Mouse's immediate backyard, there is constant fascination and temptation: a vegetable garden; woodlands filled with deer, squirrels, and rabbits; and a pond that she likes to swim in. "She's a bit scared about the grass carp fish we have put in, however," says Conran.

One of the first things Mouse enjoys when she returns from her outside excursions is to lie on her back in the front hall on a large cap cushion in red and purple. "Basically, she likes to place herself where she gets the most tummy rubs," says Conran. The house's seven bedrooms and simple grandeur allow for plenty of easy playtime and no fuss. "I wanted to keep the decor quite simple and fill it with antiques and finds from local auction houses," says Conran. "I don't want it to be too formal. It is a house that is great for lots of people and their dogs." There is plenty of entertaining on weekends in the east-facing dining room, with its icinglike cornicing, floor-to-ceiling sash windows, and large marble fireplace, which is almost always lit. Even with the room's imposing Venetian glass chandeliers and seven hand-painted Chinese panels, dogs are as much invited to the party as humans.

Conran's mother, food writer Caroline Conran, lives nearby and is a frequent guest with her dogs, Mouse's best friends Ralph, a Jack Russell, and Dolly, a rescue who is the spitting image of "Duchess" from Beatrix Potter's *The Pie and the Patty Pan*. "My mum always had a dog while I was growing up, so it is wonderful for me to have my first dog play with hers," says Conran. "Mouse is such a positive little spirit. She is part of what makes the house a home."

PREVIOUS SPREAD: Conran and Mouse descending the eighteenth-century sandstone, cantilevered staircase.

RIGHT: Conran and Mouse on the front lawn walking toward their Grade II listed home, built in the late 1700s and altered in 1807 by neoclassical architect James Wyatt. It was once owned by the Duke of Wellington.

OPPOSITE: Mouse elegantly reclines on a camelback sofa in the entrance hall with seventeenth-century Tree of Life embroideries behind her.

ABOVE: The boot room is home to Conran's fantastic collection of baskets and all manner of coats and shoes for an impromptu walk around the grounds. On the wall is Conran's flock wallpaper designed with Arthur Price.

FOLLOWING SPREAD: Mouse in the living room, her preferred spot in the winter when the fire is roaring. This room has soaring views across the gardens at the back of the house. The sofas were designed by Conran's father, Sir Terence Conran.

PAGES 196-197: The unfinished dining room with a Murano glass chandelier, hand-painted silk panels from de Gournay, and a large eighteenth-century dresser.

RIGHT: Mouse rests on her favorite ikat cushion at the front door, where she can watch the comings and goings of the household, and enthusiastically welcome visitors.

BELOW: Conran sits at her desk with a small selection from her collection of English Mocha ware bowls and mugs.

OPPOSITE: Conran and Mouse relax in the master bedroom on a bespoke four-poster bed. Another spot to hang out is on the small settee covered with Turkish silk velvet pillows.

Susie Atkinson
and Woody

DESIGNER
Susie Atkinson
Interior designer

DOG
Woody, age ten
Golden cocker spaniel

THEIR COUNTRY HOME
Hampshire, England

"THERE IS NEVER A DULL MOMENT when Woody is around, especially in the country," says Susie Atkinson, who owns a prestigious London-based design firm and counts the Soho House club both in London and Berlin as two of her many acclaimed projects. "He is known around our little hamlet of Dipley as the escape artist who is on the hunt for food. On several occasions he has even appeared at our back door with someone else's supper in his mouth. One Christmas it was Stilton cheese."

The River Whitewater drew Atkinson and her family—husband Justin and their three children—to the property. When Woody is at home in the country, this is his favorite spot. The bank is covered with snowdrops, daffodils, bluebells, and fritillary, and toward summer, wild garlic. "It is the place that both Woody and I love to be," says Atkinson. "He barks at the geese and ducks and generally loves to roll around in the grasses and the wild garlic. And, of course, after a long walk when he is hot and panting, one of his tip-top favorite things is to cool off right there in the river." Walks are taken twice a day and Woody will dramatically sing out a reminder to his family lest they forget.

Atkinson has worked continuously on the property over the nineteen years she's lived there. Outside, she has created "rooms" with different focal points, including a potager with a greenhouse and raised beds clad in willow where Woody loves to lie in the morning sun. A side paddock wraps around the drive with crab apple trees, and it is here that Woody has his own little outbuilding surrounded by a picket fence where he goes after muddy walks and spends the night. A dog flap allows him to come and go when he pleases, and a heater keeps the temperature cozy.

A front garden has been laid with York stone and planted with evergreen plants like yew and box for structure during the winter months. "After a long walk, Woody uses the yew hedges like a towel, rubbing himself along them to dry off," says Atkinson.

Inside, the 1846 house has been completely renovated, from enlarging the once small kitchen to putting in a new staircase in the central hall. "One of the most important things for me when designing our home was to fill it with light and to have as many windows as possible looking out onto the garden," says Atkinson. "I really wanted my house to flow well, to feel open and to work practically as a family home as well as being a place to entertain friends." A dilapidated barn has been transformed into an entertainment space, complete with a huge open fire and gym and is used constantly by the children. However many guests come and go, Woody, with his boundless energy, is always keen to keep up. "Woody is not a dog for the fainthearted," says Atkinson. "But we absolutely love him, noisy singing and all."

PREVIOUS SPREAD: After a long walk, Woody uses the yew hedges like a towel, rubbing himself along them to dry his coat.

LEFT: The 1846 house viewed from the river. "One of the most important things for me when renovating it was to fill it with light and to have as many windows as possible looking out onto the garden," says Atkinson. It is a welcome sight after a long ramble with Woody along the riverbank.

ABOVE: The sunny terrace is ideal for summer entertaining.

RIGHT: A decorative trellis defines a cool green space on the sunniest days.

OPPOSITE: Atkinson has filled her home with contemporary art, sourcing many pieces directly from the artists themselves. This comfy corner sofa is the perfect place for quiet contemplation, until Woody comes to claim her attention.

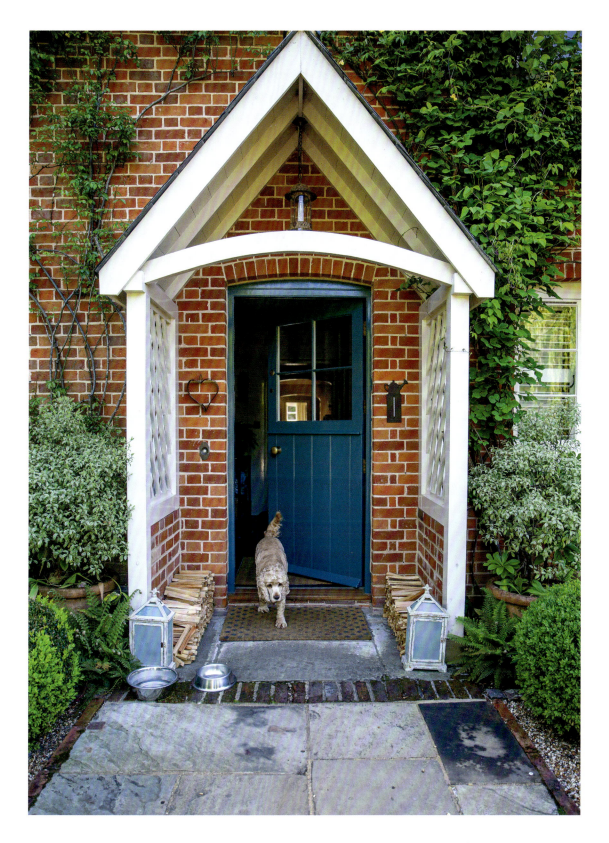

OPPOSITE: The light and spacious kitchen is the heart of Atkinson's home. Family and friends gather there on weekends for informal lunches or dinners. The kitchen table is surrounded by her Craftmaker's dining chairs, with ebonized frames and rush seats. Woody is never far from the kitchen—he likes to curl up by the AGA stove, and is always hopeful for a few bits of food to come his way.

ABOVE: Woody is known around the neighborhood as a skilled "escape artist" who, once he has finished his own dinner, will often go on the hunt for someone else's.

FOLLOWING SPREAD: The potager garden catches the morning sun. It is a favorite place for Woody to bask and watch as work progresses on the raised vegetable beds.

Veere Grenney
and Rio

DESIGNER
Veere Grenney
Interior designer

DOG
Rio, age eight
Lurcher

THEIR COUNTRY HOME
The Temple
*Stoke-by-Nayland,
Suffolk, England*

"THE HAPPIEST DOGS HAVE a routine life," says Veere Grenney. And the daily walking rituals he spends with his dog, Rio, across the countryside in Stoke-by-Nayland give no better proof. This New Zealand native begins each early summer morning like a quintessential Englishman, with a rigorous walk with his beloved lurcher at his side, followed by an almost three-hour jaunt at five p.m. In the winter, it is usually a restorative two-hour walk at midday.

Their destination is the neighboring Dedham Vale, on the borders of Essex and Suffolk. "It is where John Constable did all his great paintings," says Grenney. "We have wonderful footpaths throughout the rolling hills." No matter where they roam, Rio is alert to nature's abundance. "When she was a puppy, she could spot a rabbit almost a hundred yards away," says Grenney proudly. "Lurchers are in the group of dogs called sight hounds because they have the keenest eyesight of any other dog."

When they are not out walking, Rio stays close to Grenney with a graceful gait, as together they reap the parkland pleasures of their country retreat known as The Temple in Stoke-by-Nayland. Originally a fishing lodge on the Tendring Hall estate, which was demolished in the fifties, The Temple was built by architect Robert Taylor around 1740 after he returned to England from his studies in Rome. It reflects the golden hues of the Italian countryside. Celebrated decorator David Hicks, a mentor to Grenney, saved The Temple from demolition in the late fifties and retreated there for a time with his pug, Algy. But for the past thirty years, Grenney, and now Rio, have maintained and basked in its ethereal glow.

The house's delightfully unexpected, fairy-tale-like presence is hard to envision unless seen in person, and Grenney himself describes it best: "It faces east over the water and west over the countryside and is in perfect harmony with nature, incorporating the principles of Palladian architecture—simple, grand, country, luxurious yet altogether relaxed. It has been my ultimate refuge."

Grenney launched his own firm in 1991, after working in antiques in his twenties. He started with a stall on Portobello Road before landing his first design job with legend Mary Fox Linton before rising to become director of Colefax & Fowler. While Grenney's work now takes him from New York to the Caribbean, to the Middle East and numerous European countries, Rio resides at his London town house, which is adjacent to Hyde Park. It was specifically purchased by Grenney for its lurcher-friendly location, but there is no place he would rather be than at The Temple with his dog by his side.

When she is not tracking the paths of the Constable countryside, Rio loves to reside indoors among the pale palette of pink and grays of the upstairs grand salon, which is sparingly yet comfortably decorated with a mix of eighteenth- and nineteenth-century antiques. Some of the furnishings are upholstered in Grenney's own fabrics. Here is where they enjoy the enchanted views of the canal with its allées of pleached hornbeam stretched out below. But Rio is equally at home in the humbler cottagelike rooms below, whether sleeping on a mink blanket or in a basket.

Together Rio and Grenney host a myriad of weekend visitors, who stream to The Temple's tall white gates only sixty miles from London, yet worlds away, grateful to slumber after a blissful day in the country in the chicly converted eighteenth-century kennels. Guests are always encouraged to bring their dogs. "Rio is enormously social and there is nothing she loves more than being chased by other dogs, although very few can ever catch her," says Grenney. In the summer, dogs and their humans love swimming in the canal, except for Rio, who like all lurchers hates water so much that if it is raining, she may even skip her beloved walk. "I cannot imagine a life without a dog for any moment," says Grenney. "They become a mirror of yourself and their love and loyalty know no balance."

PREVIOUS SPREAD: Grenney and Rio relax in the pink salon at The Temple. The neoclassical fireplace mantel is always lined with personal collections and curiosities that Grenney holds dear.

LEFT: The canal can be seen from the double-hung windows of the salon. Grenney planted pleached hornbeam in the eighteenth-century manner following a huge storm in 1987 that decimated the two-hundred-year-old chestnuts, which originally lined it. In warmer months Grenney enjoys paddling there in his small rowboat as well as swimming in its waters. Rio, however, prefers to stay on the bank.

FOLLOWING SPREAD: In the grand salon the white of the ornate plaster ceiling softly contrasts with the pink of the walls below. "This palest shell pink is the most perfect color for a Palladian drawing room," says Grenney. "If it was a hall, I would do it in an off-white bone color. Here, however, the pale pink cozies up the room and allows it to feel more domestic."

RIGHT: At the entrance of the salon is a bookcase, which was designed by Grenney. Poised on its surface is a nineteenth-century French sphinx. "I love anything Egyptian," says Grenney.

BELOW: Grenney turned the property's former kennels into a shipshape guest room. "This room is only eight feet wide and therefore a pair of old-fashioned hospital beds are the perfect solution for its modest proportions," says Grenney. The walls are painted a crisp white and adorned with paintings by family and friends.

OPPOSITE: Rio peruses her options from the salon stairway. Underfoot is rush matting. "It's always the go-to floor matting in an English country house," says Grenney.

OPPOSITE: Grenney and Rio go for extensive walks each day they are in the country, exploring the footpaths throughout the rolling hills of the countryside of neighboring Dedham Vale, where The Temple is situated. "It's an area of extraordinary natural beauty," says Grenney. "It's completely restorative for both of us. And perfect rabbit country for a lurcher to hone her skills."

RIGHT: Grenney completely transformed the property by adding formal hedges and garden areas. Here, Rio poses elegantly next to some potted lemon trees. "Rio is very loyal and never wanders off, but her curiosity for a rabbit will often tempt her into the countryside that surrounds the canal," says Grenney.

BELOW, LEFT: In his locally bought greenhouse, Grenney grows approximately fifty different varieties of pelargonium, mainly in pinks to white but never red, ensuring that The Temple is always dressed up with plants growing in pots. "I first saw geraniums used extensively in Italy when I visited Harold Acton's villa outside Florence," says Grenney. "In pots only they are the perfect way to beautify a Palladian villa."

BELOW, RIGHT: Grenney's signature pink geraniums bloom in front of the oeil-de-boeuf window added by David Hicks in the sixties when he lived at The Temple. The window was designed for Hicks by the renowned English architect Raymond Erith.

FOLLOWING SPREAD: "There's a quiet formality to The Temple's surrounding gardens and hedges," says Grenney. "Rio always looks especially elegant coming or going."

Acknowledgments

Thank you to my invaluable photographer, roundabout navigator, dog whisperer, mind reader, and style soul mate Stacey Bewkes. Without you, there would not only be no book but a lot less joy in my life. I am so lucky you are by my side, taking the shot before I even think of it—no matter the time zone.

Thank you also to my wonderful editor Sandy Gilbert for taking on a whole fresh pack of dogs and their designers, in another country, no less. And to Charles Miers at Rizzoli for agreeing to usher them across the proverbial threshold.

To Kayleigh Jankowski, my inimitable art director and fellow avocado lover: you are a visual wizard.

Thank you, Elizabeth Downing, for making so many lovely introductions for us.

Dylan Bowman, I appreciate your keen eyes and big heart, not to mention delicious company on the long journey back to London post-shoots.

Miguel Flores-Vianna, besides being such a talent behind the camera, you are always as generous with your offers to help.

To the staff at Kit Kemp's Haymarket Hotel: you are the reason why we were able to do fourteen shoots in ten days, twice over. You brought us things before we even knew we needed them. You made us feel both extraordinarily at home and yet transported.

Finally, to all the beloved dogs and their humans for opening their extraordinary homes to us—thank you.

Captions

PAGE 2: Justin Van Breda and Margot near the orchard of their country home.

PAGE 4: Henrietta Courtauld and Arthur walking into the walled garden of Wardington Manor.

PAGE 6: Theo, Campbell's shitzu, advises on how to trim the kumquats in their London garden.

PAGE 8, TOP LEFT: A special Christmas present from Campbell's three youngest grandchildren (containing photographs of them by Harry Soames) is topped with a Connolly leather dog.

PAGE 8, TOP RIGHT: Artist Nathalie Lété painted Archie and Theo on plates for Campbell.

PAGE 8, BOTTOM: Campbell's desk is filled with many treasures, especially cards from stationer Mrs. John L. Strong, with her late dog Archie and Theo etched on them.

PAGE 9: Theo favors a newly made bed, and is very particular about the bed linen. "He loves Porthault, but here he's making do with vintage," says Campbell. The sheets on her bed are embroidered linen from the Monogrammed Linen Shop in London and the bedspread is a vintage tablecloth, which Campbell often uses on beds.

PAGE 10: As we approached Wardington Manor, we didn't need a GPS to know that we had come to the right place.

PAGE 11, TOP: There's no better way to meet someone than through their garden. Justin Van Breda gave me a tour of his grounds, which are just as charismatic as him.

PAGE 11, MIDDLE: Is there anything more delicious than a black pug named Dahlia wearing a custom malachite collar?

PAGE 11, BOTTOM: Whether focused on dogs or gardens, Stacey was always one stylish shot ahead of me.

PAGE 12, TOP: Carlos Sánchez-García's darling Alfred was the first dog to greet us on our journey in making *At Home in the English Countryside*. His beguiling eyes and trusting warmth was an emotional touchstone for me and set the tone for the book.

PAGE 12, MIDDLE: No one picks from a garden's bounty quite like the Brits.

PAGE 12, BOTTOM: During our shoot at Christopher Howe's, I checked in with my own dogs in America while Apollo made me feel right at home.

PAGE 13: We never unpacked our rain hats or boots the entire trip. Stacey photographed Bunny Guinness and her pups on a glorious sunny day.

PAGE 223: Gobi and Abbi wait patiently by the front door for Penny Morrison to go for a walk through the nearby bluebell woods. Leashes and walking sticks are at the ready.

Portrait Textile Credits

PAGES 14-15: Aristoloche Anselm from Watts of Westminster

PAGES 26-27: Soane Britain's Espalier Square Linen in Emerald

PAGES 42-43: March Hare, design by Jane Churchill fabrics and wallpapers. Photo courtesy of Cowtan & Tout, Inc. All rights reserved.

PAGES 54-55: Tree Peony from Robert Kime

PAGES 70-71: Thimble Print Linen, 'Little Weed' in Mauve from 36 Bourne Street

PAGES 84-85: Milton in Bleu Vert from Claremont

PAGES 94-95: Point de Hongrie by Edmond Petit Fabrics, represented by Turnell & Gigon Group UK

PAGES 110-111: Batik Raisin in Vert from Le Manach

PAGES 120-121: The Passion and The Glory in Natural, from The Katherine Amies Collection by Justin Van Breda

PAGES 132-133: Dogs Socialising by Domenica More Gordon from Chelsea Textiles

PAGES 140-141: Moondog in Fuchsia Pink by Kit Kemp for Chelsea Textiles

PAGES 152-153: Greuze in Bleu Rouge by Pierre Frey Le Manach

PAGES 162-163 AND ENDPAPERS: Aurora on Nivelles Oyster Linen in Green, by Paolo Moschino for Nicholas Haslam Ltd.

PAGES 176-177: Killi Blue by Penny Morrison

PAGES 188-189: Lingonberry in Red by Sophie Conran

PAGES 200-201: Jungle Birds in Light Blue, by Marthe Armitage Prints Limited

PAGES 210-211: Temple in Pink by Veere Grenney Collection

Please note that the featured dogs' ages reflect the time that they were photographed, between Fall 2018 and Spring 2019.

First published in the United States of America in 2020 by Rizzoli International Publications, Inc.
300 Park Avenue South
New York, NY 10010
www.rizzoliusa.com

Publisher: Charles Miers
Editor: Sandy Gilbert
Design: Kayleigh Jankowski
Production Manager: Alyn Evans
Editorial Assistance: Kelli Rae Patton, Sara Pozefsky, Hilary Ney
Managing Editor: Lynn Scrabis

Printed in China

2020 2021 2022 2023 / 10 9 8 7 6 5 4 3 2

ISBN: 978-0-8478-6478-2
Library of Congress Control Number: 2019953111

Visit us online:
Facebook.com/RizzoliNewYork
instagram.com/rizzolibooks
twitter.com/Rizzoli_Books
pinterest.com/rizzolibooks
youtube.com/user/RizzoliNY
issuu.com/Rizzoli